HAUNTED TOWNS: GHOST STORIES OF NEWFOUNDLAND AND LABRADOR

By Geraldine Ryan-Lush

Mulberry Books 2019

ISBN 978-0-9947339-8-6

Cover Photo: *Train Station In Avondale.* Photo Credit: Geraldine Ryan-Lush (C) Copyright Geraldine Ryan-Lush 2019

Cover Design By Geraldine Ryan-Lush

$19.95 CDN

For Don, my balance.

Acknowledgements

Just as the smell of paint takes me immediately back to childhood and Christmas, when the kitchen of my St. Mary's Bay home would be painted , along with a new laying of linoleum for the festive season, so does the smell of woodsmoke in the Fall evoke vivid memories of turnips carved out for Hallowe'en. They take me back to the long evenings of kerosene lamps, visiting neighbours, and woodstove heat. The pungent, acrid smell of burnt turnip Jack O' Lanterns glowing with melted candle wax is a haunted feast for the senses that could never be matched. They   lit our way down the sea-kissed lanes and dark-as-pitch gravel roads, as we made our precarious way trick-or-treating in homemade Hallowe'en costumes, occasionally spiced up with a sweaty plastic mask from the Arcade in St. John's.

I grew up with my feet stuck in the oven in the vast wood, coal, and oil range, reading. How good it felt to come in from risking life and limb sliding belly buster on steep hills that held no mercy once you were on them: you either banged into a stable or a fence, or you didn't. It was a fait accompli. I skated on frozen ponds miles in the woods, and jumped off wharves, swimming in the frigid Salmonier Arm. The kitchen was the warmest room in the house, and the richest for a little girl with big ears. That, and the iron, checkered heat grate in the upstairs hallway , which sported my prone flushed face many times, as I strained to hear hair-raising ghost stories not meant for childish ears. I don't have my feet stuck in the oven anymore, or my face scorched from the grate, but I'm still addicted to books and stories, especially the bone-chilling and unexplained variety. Heartfelt thanks to my many friends and colleagues (you know who you are), who shared, or at least put up with, in a generous way, my passion for a good story.

   Posthumous Acknowledgements to my parents, Gabriel and Kathleen Ryan, recently departed, and my grandparents, Jerome and Elizabeth Ryan, James Benedict Power and Mary "Stannie"
Power, long gone; as well, to the kindly neighbours and friends , the

kitchen raconteurs, who in oilcloth sheen and kettle song, gave me the foundation for what would become a long and successful writing career, feeding my eager soul for time immemorial.

INTRODUCTION

St. John's, Newfoundland, is reputed to be the oldest city in North America. 500 years young , to be exact. It is North America's most easterly city. Existing on maps since 1519, it is one of the oldest, if not the oldest European settlements in North America. It has a rich history, having played a part in the Seven Year War, the French and Indian War, the American Revolutionary War, and the War of 1812. It has been almost annihilated by fire several times, most famously by the Great Fire of 1892. A tragic fire at the hands of German espionage, killing 99 military and civilian, from all stripes, the Knights of Columbus Hostel Fire, happened in this city in 1942. During World War Two, the harbour supported Royal Navy and Royal Canadian Navy ships that were engaged in anti-submarine warfare. It is also the site of an American Air Force Base at Fort Pepperrell.

With such an old and rich history, St. John's has known its share of piracy, murder on the high seas, port brawls between foreign seamen and locals, tragedies by fire, death and disease, shipwrecks, enemy torpedoes, hangings, torture in stockades, and the like. No wonder so much has been written about the gruesome, ghostly lore of old St. John's. Over the centuries and in recent decades, numerous stories have been told, retold, written about, and filmed, dealing with the paranormal visitations, and unyielding revenge on our frozen, isolated shores, by vicious or friendly apparitions, depending on the setting and circumstances. I myself have had a ghost book published recently, a work of fiction , *Hannigan's Hand,* with a true story of a shipwreck not far from St. John's, and cursed revenge , as its genesis.

As a child growing up in the heart of the Irish Loop, ninety minutes from St. John's, in St. Mary's Bay, Newfoundland, I was part of a genuine storytelling culture, complete with kerosene oil lamps and no television as my daily ritual. *Hannigan's Hand* stemmed from an old memory of a neighbour's true encounter with a headless man on a beach. Following the encounter, the man's hand became blood-poisoned, or "fairy-blasted," and the local priest had to perform something of an exorcism on the man, who had been cursed by the spirits of a shipwreck whose territory he had invaded. The story was told over and over in our St. Joseph's kitchen, and settled in my psyche as a true horror story, the full true incident being related as one of the stories in this book. My own father, Lance Corporal Gabriel Ryan of the Newfoundland Militia, was a survivor of the horrendous Knights Of Columbus Fire of 1942. The story of he and his brother Larry having been saved from the trapped flames by his mother's premonition in her bay kitchen that terrible night has been well documented in published sources as a mystery of paranormal tones. A book about my father and his heroism in that fire, *His Soldier's Coat: Gabriel Ryan And The Knights Of Columbus Fire Of 1942* , written by my son, Shannon Marshall Lush, is also published, available worldwide, and is in most public libraries.

The stories of old have been written out, or will they ever be written out, given our culture, history, and appetite for the unknown, the macabre and mysterious. I possess a rich cache of the old fodder, stemming from my orally-rich background, and some of this is included in this book. But it's the modern paranormal happenings which enthrall me now.

By this enlightened time in our foggy, mist-covered, rugged Isle, the general perception seems to be that no ghostly activity exists here now, or if it does exist, it's only in the mind of the teller. Skeptics abound in this New Millennium, and a sensible person with a decent job and family to provide for, is hardly likely to be caught dead , pardon the pun, spilling in his lunchroom or the local Tim Horton's the fact he had witnessed something out of the ordinary, something he had seen with his own two eyes in broad daylight, and with a witness to boot. He would be escorted out the door of his employment quite politely, his services no longer needed, and his fellow witness in tow.

But the truth remains that rampant paranormal activity is happening all the time in Newfoundland towns and cities,   albeit only whispered about in close circles. In the following pages I shall attempt to present these true stories, some having occurred as recently as winter 2018. The stories are true. The names have been changed, at the request of the subjects' wish for privacy.   Stories told to me personally by subjects who didn't want to be identified are rendered in the third person, with quotes from the subject. All of these stories are true and original, coming from my own cache of luckily, a lifetime well of experience in the old and new, Newfoundland folklore culture I was raised in. They were not culled from the books or collections of others; but in the true oral tradition, the only real tradition of storytelling. I did, of course, use some scholarly research to add perspective to some of the stories from a historical viewpoint. These sources are cited at the end of this book.

 Most interesting is the ongoing activity at a production plant in Pleasantville, which reportedly was once a morgue in a military building I shall number the "301," during the First and Second World Wars, and beyond. The "301," as a production plant, is made up of several large sections. One is a storage/supply area , where workers gamely go at dead of night to get a tool needed for a repair/maintenance job on some machinery they are working on, to keep the plant up and running for next day's production. Another is a lunchroom, well lit by day and night, servicing the 300 or so employees on their breaks. The "301," although an old building, doesn't look like a ghost house, but a ghost house it is. Once a new employee, oblivious to the chilling history of it, is asked by a foreman to go over to the storage/supply area at 3 A.M. to get a part, oft times comes back ashen-faced and weak, saying nothing of why he is in that state, but thereafter refusing to go near the place again, unless he is accompanied, and if they both see something, the pledge of secrecy is made. Men of 65 and 70 years old, having worked at this facility for 40 or 50 years, in the midst of animated conversation at work, clam up and look strange, if asked about the history of the place. They have blocked from their psyche their experiences, and no amount of coaxing and wheedling will draw them from their protective shell. This production plant facility, being in Pleasantville, is also part of the site of Fort Pepperrell, the American built base during the duration of WW2. Pleasantville was also a training ground for soldiers preparing to embark overseas, and the Newfoundland Regiment and Militia/ Home Guard. Several of the ghost stories coming out of this facility center around the witnessing and residual hauntings of many soldiers, especially one worker who witnessed a full body apparition of a soldier many times. This worker, refusing to be undaunted, kept his silence. However, he went back time after time on matters relating to his work, only to be confronted with the same soldier, whom he could describe right down to the colour of his hair and uniform, his tidy, black moustache, and the fact he looked at him out of intent, puzzled eyes. The full stories of the soldier ghost, and the other horrific hauntings in this production plant will be dealt with in forthcoming chapters.

Other stories in this collection concern everything from a deceased taxi driver who refused to leave his earthly cabbie after it was sold, to a woman who was visited by her dead father during an "old hag" episode, saving her life when she was unable to come awake. Also, a thrift store ceiling fixture which light bulbs kept burning for 5 years without burning out. Dopplegangers and Crisis Apparition stories are also grist for the mill in this collection. The stories are varied, and creepy, and most of all, true. They happened to sane, intelligent, objective people who, prior to the encounters, had laughed off paranormal activities. And they happened, and are happening mere months ago, and in the present, in this old city, and environs. Clearly, the cities and towns of Newfoundland continue to be beloved, by the living and the dead, to infinity.

CONTENTS

Stranger In The Graveyard

She Didn't Like Me

Let There Be Light...And Light...And Light

True Stories From Gabriel Ryan (*The Ghost Of Mickey Quinn*) (*Poor Malachy Needs A Prayer*)

The Man On The Rock: What The Police Officer Saw

The Angry Ghost Of St. Patrick's Church

The Curse Of Thomas Mackey

The Strange Premonition Of Elizabeth Ryan

Haunting In The Attic: Twillingate

The Ghost In The Cell Phone

The Ghost On The Bridge

She Walks At Midnight In High Heels

Terror In A White Horse

The Black Blanket

Saved By A Dead Father's Voice

The Stolen Child

The Doppleganger or The Fetch

Phone Call From The Other Side

Crisis Apparitions: (Sheila's Story) (Diane's Story)

Grandmother Came To Say Goodbye

The Ghostly Truck Starter

Steve Bragg, St. John's born and bred, and Joe Walsh, a native of Trinity Bay but working in St. John's, were good friends and co-workers. In their 40's , married with families, they did not often get a chance to embark on a hunting or fishing trip outside the city, but whenever they did, they enjoyed it with gusto. One sunny summer weekend in 2017, they packed up their ATV's and gear in Joe's pick-up, and headed out to Trinity Bay for some salmon fishing. Driving through the main road in the community of Port Rexton, about 3 P.M., the sun blaring overhead, Joe's pick-up suddenly stopped. Joe was perplexed. A full tank of gas, a tune-up, pristine tires, a new pick-up practically off the store ramp, he couldn't figure out what was wrong. He turned the key futilely, nothing happened. Not a sound. So it wasn't the battery, or anything he could point a finger at. Steve was stumped as well. Together they got out and investigated, wondering what had made the dependable F-350 come to a sudden, abrupt stop in the middle of the road, and refuse to start again. They were not a little embarrassed, as other motorists were passing them on the road, casting glances in their direction. No one offered to help though, which Joe remarked to Steve was strange, in this neck of the woods in Newfoundland, or any part of Newfoundland, particularly the outports, where friendliness

9

and helpfulness reigned supreme.

Puzzled and frustrated at this turn of events, they got back in the pick-up where Joe continued to turn the key every few minutes with no result. Not a gig. They weren't ready to hunt for a garage yet though, and decided to wait it out for awhile. It was just something simple they were missing, it had to be. Suddenly, they heard footsteps approaching in the gravel to the side of the pavement, and a hearty male voice called out in the bay vernacular, "Having some trouble are ye?" They looked up, and a smiling, pleasant man of around their age was standing at the drivers' side open window. He poked his head in, fiddled with the gears, and all of a sudden the engine was running good as new. "There now, she's all clear. She'll be fine now." Their amiable benefactor declared. Steve and Joe cheered in unison, and looked up to thank the smiling man, wondering what the heck he did, and what the matter had been with the stubborn truck. They were looking at air. There was nothing or no one there, where a mini fraction of a second before there had been. They stared at each other. They leapt out of the pick-up, refusing to believe what had transpired. There was not a soul in sight the length of the pavement, or to the skirt of it, which extended in a straight line for some goodly way, and for which they had a clear view. There was no way he could have disappeared like that, talking one second, gone the next, without them knowing.

 The two men stood on the road, not wanting to let on to the other that cold shivers were running up their spine on this hot June day. Finally Joe spoke. "Let's go to the garage. I haven't been there in years, all new owners, but I'm going to get her checked out before we go any further." Steve knew Joe simply wanted answers of some kind. They took the kitten-purring pick-up in to the local garage. A mechanic came back with the diagnosis, after Joe had instructed him to give her a good going over: The truck was running perfect, not a sign of anything wrong anywhere, and there shouldn't be any problems. Pale-faced, Joe told him about the breakdown and the disappearing stranger who miraculously got the truck going again. Quietly the mechanic looked them both in the eye. "What did he look like?" Steve gave the description of the friendly man. "Whereabouts did the truck break down?" Joe gave him as near an estimate as he could as to where the truck had stalled and refused to budge. The mechanic lowered his head and stopped for a moment. When he looked up he had a sad, knowing look on his knitted, grease-spotted brow. "That was Mike Hanrahan. He was killed in that very spot three years ago. You're not the first he has helped out." He slowly went back to his work. Steve and Joe carried on with their fishing trip, the truck running perfectly. They were more subdued than previous trips, and when they got back to St. John's to work, it was weeks before they could sleep through the night. Joe especially, who had been in the driver's side and remembers every detail of the friendly stranger, continues to be haunted by the voice and face of the pleasant helper, who, not resting in peace and needing camaraderie, continues to assist road travellers from the confines of his too-early grave which he was placed in after departing this earthly realm so tragically.

THE GIRL ON THE ROAD

26-year-old Kyle Evans lived and worked in St. John's, but was dating a girl from Petty Harbour-Maddox Cove, a picturesque community of 960 people about twenty minutes drive from the city. Nestled in Motion Bay, just south of St. John's, the town is 200 years old, and occupied since 1598, making it one of the oldest European settlements in North America. For centuries dependent on the fishing trade, with the cod moratorium of 1992, tourism is now the staple industry, with people flocking to the town to enjoy the beautiful scenery, the quaintness, the icebergs, the whales , the culturally quaint restaurant Chafe's Landing, and the hiking trails. Also a popular area for television and films, it has been the site of many and varied productions, of world and international acclaim.

Feeling leisurely and relaxed this fine September evening in 2015, Kyle decided to take the old Maddox Cove Road as his route, even though other veins and highways from the capital city were more modern and populated. Maddox Cove Road is a spooky stretch of road in the best of weather, and had it been foggy, as it is most often in the area, Kyle would have had second thoughts. The old road had become infamous back in 1980, when the body of a murdered young girl,   had been found in the woods off the road, by a couple in search of a Christmas tree. Bare, and bordered on each side by scruff and scrappy spruce trees and wild , weedy growths, it is not populated much as a traveller's route, but often a less-policed road in recent years, making it a bit of a drag-racing area. Local police are seldom seen here, tending to focus their energies on the more demanding Metro, unless of course a crime or emergency happens. None of this was bothering Kyle Evans however, this bright evening about an hour from dusk as he set off to visit his girlfriend Karen in Petty Harbour.

He remembers the details of that evening vividly, culminating in his arriving at his girlfriend's father's door in a state of near collapse. It was about 6:00 P.M., and he was driving not in a hurried fashion, when he noticed something on the road up ahead of him. Getting closer, he drew a gasp. There was a person, a young woman sitting there, in the middle of the pavement, just staring straight at him. "Jesus," he thought. "What the hell is SHE doing there! Is she trying to get killed, trying to end it all?" His first instinct when he saw her there was to stop, and take care of her, as he saw what he believed to be a young woman either physically paralysed or sick, or mentally deranged enough that she wanted to kill herself. He slammed on the brakes. It was at this moment that his heart dropped to his stomach, as, nausea gripping him in shock, he perceived the woman rising up from her sitting position on the pavement, like the Holy Ghost ascending into heaven. She was lifting up from the pavement , full featured and reddish-brown hair , her whole body flowing over the hood of the car, and right through the windshield, disintegrating into cloudy nothingness, her thin arms shot out in front of her, as she draped over the headrests and backseats and out the back window.

Kyle was immobile for about 15 minutes, in shock at what he had just witnessed. His breathing was labored, and he was breaking out in a cold sweat all over his body. He pulled the car over to the side, tried to get some contol over himself. He had to call Karen, make some excuse as to why he was late. His fingers fumbled uselessly on the phone. "My God," he thought. "Am I having a heart attack? A stroke?" He knew what he had seen. She was real. Flesh and blood real. Her features swam before his eyes, contorted in some sheer mental anquish. He had never seen anything like it in his life before, the way she had come up from the road, glided in over the hood and out through the windshield. Such things only had been witnessed in movies with special effects, but there were no movie people here, or no special effects, on this lonely, gloomy old road which was getting colder and foggier with every second.

Kyle didn't know if he was able to drive or not. He was scared to drive, he was scared to move or do anything. Whatever that was, whoever SHE was, she was still inside his car. That nothingness, that form, was still there, inside his car. He could feel her presence: he was freezing, the car was freezing, and not just from the fog. But he had to get her out somehow. In his shocked state he desperately opened the windows, he turned on the defrost, he wanted to get out and leave the doors open, to waft out the spirit, but it was turning ever colder and he was wearing only a T-shirt, the bipolar weather of Newfoundland making a fool of him again that day as he started off in the warm sun. He got out anyway, and stood there on the side of the road, car doors swung open, windows down. "Jesus," he thought, shivering violently. "I'm going to catch pneumonia." What would anyone passing think? A sudden thought assailed him. The trunk! Maybe she, the form, the girl, was in the trunk! She had come in through the windshield after all, and out through the backseats. Maybe she was going to hang around for awhile. Maybe he would never get rid of her. "Maybe I should just leave the damn car here, " he thought desperately. He opened the trunk to let it air out. He hoped no cops in police cars or passersby would see him, standing there in the fog scantily clad, car doors swinging open, windows down, trunk up. They would be on him like blood hounds, thinking he had a dead body, a murdered body in the trunk.

"I wasn't able to drive," He said. "I was too traumatized. I didn't know how I was going to get to Karen's or even back home. And I couldn't tell her, I couldn't tell her father, he would think I was doing ecstasy or crack cocaine or something which was the rage a few years ago, even though I wasn't into it. It wasn't my game. " Eventually, the sub-arctic cold and fog forced him back into the car, and he started out and somehow made his way into Petty Harbour, pleading a sudden stomach virus or food poisoning as the reason for his collapsed state. But 2 years later, he cringes at the memory of that terrible night, following which he missed several shifts of work and had a future father- in- law eyeing him with a wary eye. He is convinced it was a tragic spirit there on the road, gone before her time. And he also thinks he may have a theory as to who the ghost might have been. The talk at his workplace was that there had been a woman in her twenties killed on that road a year before. She had just purchased a car from a private seller, who assured her the workings were fine. The car was actually faulty, but the crooked seller didn't tell her that. The tragedy had made the local news. Kyle, waiting until he was well over his initial shock, perused the back newspaper stories until he found the story. To his horror, but not really surprising, the date the girl had met her tragic end was a year to the day he had seen the phantom , swooping mermaid-like up from the pavement and into his car. He now lights a candle for the soul of the girl , or whomever it was, who had sought him out in the depths of her tortured wanderings, in search of peace.

Was the shooting-star spectre a product of an overactive imagination, and the urban legends begun with the murder of that young girl found in the woods off Maddox Cove in the 1980's? Kyle Evans is convinced it was not. "I know what I saw," he says. "There were a few smash-ups up on that road over the years. And a few drownings. She was one of them."

Not Such A Bargain

Everyone knows that thrift stores are not just for penny-pinching Grandmas anymore. The outlets have risen in popularity over the years, and not just for economy sake, but for the uniqueness of the finds.   A jaunt to a thrift store is always a pleasure due to the element of surprise it affords, and for the creative, artistic , fashionable mind, possibilities abound.

Vivien Dunne and her husband Mark enjoy browsing in thrift stores. In St. John's, their haunts are the local Value Village, The Salvation Army Thrift Store, The S.P.C.A. Thrift Stores, where they also donate, and a few antique stores downtown.   At least once every couple of weeks or so, the couple can be found first enjoying a breakfast out at Cora's on Kenmount Road; and then up the street a little to the local Value Village, usually on Senior's Day, which allows them to keep an extra 30% of their purchases in their pocket. Sometimes they drive downtown to the antique stores dotting Water Street, but they have become selective about the age and history of their purchases for good reason, as the following chilling true story illustrates:

Mark has an affinity for old portrait photography , and he pays special attention to the frames. "Often I buy for the frames alone. I used to work at a high-end photography store before digital took over, and it's a dying art. I like to keep it alive." He states. Keeping it alive is a bit of a misnomer however in this instance, as he found out when he became attracted to a large, 16X20 inch , turn-of-the-century 1900's portrait hanging on the wall of a long-time downtown antiques store four years ago. It was an exclusive- only- to-- the rich, high-end studio portrait of two children, a boy and a girl, dressed in the period clothes of the day. They seemed well-off, and in keeping with the serious importance of such an act, were no doubt carefully prepared for the pose by family members. The children, around seven or eight, most probably siblings, the girl sitting, the boy standing, gazed at the camera in a focused, unsmiling way, their large eyes unwavering and dutiful. The name of the photography company in Boston was imprinted on the back. Mark haggled with the owner of the store who knew him well, and the couple walked out with their treasure, and it was a treasure, at the joyfully exorbitant price of $50.

Once home, they set to having it hung. Mark wanted to hang it directly over the sofa in the living room. Viven, not as passionate about antiques as her husband, and being leery of two pairs of intense 1900's eyes following her around, with memories of old ancestors peering from the walls of her grandparents' house, would much rather the portrait be placed in the rec room, or a spare bedroom . But she acquiesced to Mark, who seemed so excited over the find, caressing the frame and exclaiming over the quality of the portrait itself, and 19th century cameras as a whole. He hung the portrait carefully , using strong wire and heavy holders, with no chance of the picture ever falling from its perch save for a hurricane or other natural disaster.

For a few days all was normal, and Vivien got used to the incongruity of the old portrait , so visually arresting in its focal point over the sofa, as opposed to the other modern family photos and landscape paintings scattered about. Then, one day a week later, Mark awoke to a loud bang, and coming out to the living room, was surprised to see the portrait on the floor. It was not scratched or damaged which seemed strange, given the height it had fallen from, and the heaviness of it. He did not think it too remiss however, merely assuming that his diligence in hanging it simply was not enough. He had to do better. "When I put it back up," he said, "It was not meant to come down a second time."

Back went the solemn- looking children for the second time, secured by hooks strong enough to hold a car, let alone a picture. All was well, and Mark, in a retrospective mood with his favorite VOWR songs playing on a Saturday night, would sometimes catch himself studying the portrait from his recliner chair opposite, idly wondering who the children were, and if they ever had any real fun, or got those expensive clothes dirty. They sure looked like they weren't having much fun on that picture, he thought to himself with a wry smile. Sometimes he got a little unnerved with the way those large, penetrating eyes seemed to follow him all around, but he had heard that was the way with all old pictures; it was just in his head. After a few weeks the portrait blended in with all else in the house, and Mark and Vivien simply failed to notice it, unless a conversation piece when someone visited.   Until one night after a hard day landscaping, when Vivien was out of province visiting a sister. Mark was lying back on the sofa watching television, chunks of white cheese and a plate of crackers beside him on the coffee table. He dozed off for just a minute, and was suddenly brought back to awareness by a noise. Something had hit the door of the kitchen, then dropped to the tile floor. He heard it a second time, and his eyes flew to pieces of something flying through the air. He got up and went to the kitchen door. There, on the floor, were several pieces of the white cheese which he had cut up in chunks and placed on a plate on the coffee table for a snack. Thinking there must be some logical explanation he sat back down on the sofa. Right before his eyes , more chunks of cheese kept flying from the plate , sailing through the air, and hitting the kitchen wall, coming to rest on the kitchen floor. Mark went to the fridge and opened a beer. "What the hell is going on, " he thought. Nothing like that had ever happened before. He looked at the portrait of the two children. It was slanted. He waited for five minutes and looked again. It was slanted more, moving very slowly on its own, and listing to the side like a ship in a storm. But there was no storm or winds, no domestic dogs or cats, no explanation for any of this bizarre activity.

He put it out of his mind as best he could with another beer and went to bed. No use calling anyone, they would only laugh and tell him he was a hoot, and how many beer did he have. When Vivien came back, nothing was said. Until one night , having a quiet late supper, they heard voices. The voices of children. They were talking, laughing, and playing, their running, gaily footsteps beating a joyous, resounding path in the flowers circling the lawn. Mark and Vivien looked outside. They went outside, all around the house. No children around. Regular children would be home now , ten o'clock at night, and a school night too. But the talking , playing phantom children continued, every night, the voices daringly coming close to their kitchen window. When Vivien and Mark looked out, no one was there. When they went out, no one was there. Then something happened that was the final straw. Mark heard Vivien scream one morning.

When he went out, there was the portrait, having seemingly fallen from the Fort Knox perch it had been fastened to, and was now resting on the floor of a bedroom three rooms down. "I didn't put it there." A white-faced Vivien gasped. "And I certainly didn't." said Mark.

"We were both visibly shaken." He said. "How did the portrait fall from the wall for one thing, when there were enough bolts into it to hold a house, and there is no way it could have ended up in the bedroom three rooms down unless by human hands. And no human hands were here, except mine and my wife's. We were asleep, with no thoughts of moving anything." Neither one of them were into ghosts, or knew the difference between a residual haunting, full body apparitions, or poltergeists. But Mark had an instinctive thought that this was poltergeist activity, and negative forces were at work which could be dangerous. Going online, and doing some research into ghostly activity and poltergeists, it didn't take him long to remove the portrait and tuck it away far out of reach in the shed outside, until it could be sold.   Following his moving the portrait, the children's voices no longer could be heard, and there was no more weird activity in the house.   It was clear that these two genteel children from another century didn't quite fancy the modest, cluttered bungalow of Mark and Vivien , and perhaps are still wandering the earth in thrift stores and antique shops, searching for some semblance of their aristocratic roots, all the while being sold at bargain prices to those who unwittingly want a piece of haunted class.

THE PRODUCTION PLANT HAUNTINGS: PLEASANTVILLE

Pleasantville is a neighbourhood in the east end of St. John's, extending from the north side of Quidi Vidi Lake northward to Newfoundland Drive. It is the former site of the U.S. military base, Fort Pepperrell, built in 1941. Stories of hauntings and various paranormal activities have been coming out of Pleasantville for decades. Paramount in these stories is the repeated rumour that one of the production plant facilities there was once a morgue, used during the two world wars and beyond. My research turned up nothing in documented evidence to corroborate this , therefore I can only narrate orally-told accounts which are sworn to be true. There is strength in numbers, and many employees have witnessed and experienced chilling things. Security cameras don't lie either. The accounts are ongoing and active, the most recent occurring but a few months ago in the winter of 2018.   The production plant at the centre of these horrific tales is in the old military building, previously a morgue, which I have numbered the "301."

Phantom Footsteps And Other-Worldly Smells

A new Commissionaire in the 301 plant who was filling in for the regular patrol, was doing her rounds one night, and heard someone walking behind her on the steps. The footsteps were loud and clunking. She also smelled a strange smell that could only be compared to a bottle of Old Spice that had been in a musty place for some time. She immediately turned around to see who it was. No one was there.

Bathroom Break-ins And Lunchroom Visits

This area is also used as a lunch room. A group of workers, day shift, were eating lunch there one day. The knob on the door started turning quite aggressively. The room was securely bolted, and padlocked, with no one in there but the workers, and no way to gain access from outside. A woman sent over at night saw shadows of another person, and felt overcome by the presence of someone else. One night a female worker went to the washroom. While she was inside, the door handle began to turn quite frantically. Thinking it was a fellow worker needing to "go" rather urgently, or some other emergency, she rushed to open it. No one was there, and there was no time for anyone to escape without being seen, as there was a full view of the stairs and short landing from where she stood.

There have been numerous cases of workers hearing bangs, hammering, loud noises, whisperings, people laughing and talking, music. Several have experienced rapid taps on their shoulder, from unseen human hands while working alone at night. A worker was retrieving something from his locker one night, when the door of another locker, a few rows down, suddenly flew open on its own, with a loud bang. The worker was frightened, as there was no one there, and no explanation for the sudden poltergeist-like activity. Workers have felt extreme chills for no reason, explaining the sensation as "freezing cold going right through them."

Shadow People

The diligent Commissionaires at this plant have their work cut out for them night and day, as , at any given time their high tech cameras doing sweeps of the building have picked up unexplained shadow people . Subsequent searches only result in bafflement and bewilderment. Loud footsteps have been heard numerous times, invisible footsteps walking behind workers as they attempt to do their job. A Commissionaire was patrolling around one night when he saw two shadows of a man in a white lab coat. The shadows also showed up on his high-definition security cameras.   It is suspected it could be a fellow worker who had died sometime before.

THE SOLDIER GHOSTS OF PLEASANTVILLE

No ghost , however, is more worthy of intrigue than the Soldier ghosts of this same production plant facility in Pleasantville, as described in the introduction to this book, and preceding chapters. As stated , rampant paranormal activity has been going on in this plant for decades. This building was reportedly once a morgue, and constructed in the early 1900's, plyed its macabre trade during the First and Second World Wars and beyond. Workers have heard loud bangs, music, talking, laughter, on solo trips in the wee hours in all sections of the building, which are impossible to access from the outside due to heavy security. Electricity has gone on and off for no logical reason, shutting down operations and delaying production time for hours, to the consternation of management. Loud footsteps clomp heavily around invisibly. Locker doors have flown open. Female workers on a visit to the washrooms in the middle of the day have found themselves unable to get back out , having been locked inside by the doors suddenly slamming shut by an invisible presence. With this trepidation in their workplace, they make sure their cell phones are with them at all times. More than once a new worker, innocent to the stories, will ask another worker to accompany him on a work order, to the storage part of the 301, only to be shocked at the answer: "Not going over there, b'y. That place is haunted." One proud and lost soldier ghost has been wandering the halls, shipping areas and hydraulic systems of the plant for decades. It is suspected he has been seen by many, who, through their own trauma, and fear of reprisal by the company have kept silent. All except John Mahoney, a calm and collected millwright who, after many sightings, was able to put his initial shock and fears aside in order to systematically determine who this soldier was , or at least what era and war he was trapped in, and why he was there.

The first time John Mahoney saw the mysterious soldier it was in the shipping area of the facility. He went outside to turn hydraulics on, around 1 A.M. one night. There is an alarm door, so impossible for someone from outside to get in or out. The ghost of a soldier was standing by the garage door, just standing and looking at him. He had a rifle on his shoulder, helmet, "tied up" black or brown boots, and he made eye contact from about 10-15 feet away. He had a moustache. Trying to keep his wits about him, John phoned the Commissionaire on duty. He said he did see a shadow, but could not pick anything else up on the cameras. No one else was there. The soldier had a short , dark moustache, looked down, looked up and never spoke. He turned his head a few times, looking to the right and left. He wore a puzzled expression, as though he were lost and trying to find something or someone. John, high up on the shipping door, couldn't really tell how tall the soldier was.

John, a private man, thought it best to keep the weird encounter to himself. After a couple of days with troubled sleep, he told his wife, who seemed a little freaked, so he decided to keep mum on future sightings. He would like to not have to go to the pumps or hydraulic rooms, but it being part of his job he had no choice. The second sighting occurred in the back door of the hydraulic room, or pump room. The place was fully lit with fluorescent lighting. It was 4 A.M. John had to go over to turn the pumps off. He was bending down, working the controls. When he straightened up and turned around, there was the soldier again, standing just a few feet away.   No human could get in due to the security alarm, so this was no game or a dress-up. This time John could see more detail: a water bottle clipped to his side, gas mask on chest, rifle placed across shoulders. On his head was a round helmet . He wore a khaki uniform, and sported a neat and tidy "curly" moustache, in John's words, or what was commonly called a handlebar in previous decades.   He was dark in complexion, but Caucasian. He looked to be anywhere from 28 to 40 years old. He was clearly visible as a full man; no mist or cloudlight swirled around him, he was the same as a real person. He wore black boots. He also had what seemed to be a whistle strung around his neck and hanging down on his chest. John stared at him, and he looked back at him, again a puzzled expression on his greyish- pallored face. In a horrified fascination, John kept staring at him, until finally there was nothing. He was gone.

After he had seen him for a third time, in the pump room at 4 A.M., and they had stared at each other, John decided that next time he would gather up his shaken nerve and speak to the ghost. He would ask him, "Who are you?" and "What do you want?"

 Unfortunately, or fortunately, he did not get the chance. The soldier never reappeared to John, at least not in full body. John did have a few more frightening encounters. While standing in the midst of a job one night alone, he clearly felt taps on his shoulder by human hands. There was not a person there, but someone , or some entity, had tapped him three times on his shoulder. However, the soldier ghost never did reappear, and John did not know if he were the same one, or one of a group of military, ghostly soldiers who others in the plant had seen, and which had been the subject of secrecy and fear for so many years.   It would not end there, however. John decided to do some research.

  What he found sent chills up his spine. He had always been a reader, and had a rudimentary knowledge of both world wars. He had a layman's knowledge of some of the activity around Newfoundland's shores during World War Two. The island was a strategic location around the Allied war effort, and thus was more desired by German saboteurs, who had a goal to cripple Canada's chances any way they could. Newfoundland lay across the vital trans-Atlantic convoy routes that supported the Allied war effort. Allied ships navigated these paths to bring vital supplies to Britain, but were often attacked by roving packs of German U-boats. Newfoundland was surrounded by "Dangerous Waters." Bell Island, an island located off the Avalon Peninsula in Conception Bay , is an area of 34 square kilometers . It can be accessed by a ferry in about 20-30 minutes. Its population use the ferry every day for work and travel to St. John's. During World War Two, the mines on Bell Island supplied ore to Cape Breton's steel mills. If Germany interrupted this flow of ore, Canada's war output could be seriously affected. During World War Two , off Bell Island, the anchorage for bulk carriers shipping iron ore was attacked by German U-boats in two attacks in the fall of 1942. On September 05, 1942, the *SS Lord Strathacona* and *SS Saganaga* were attacked, and on November 02, the *Rose Castle.* Four ships were sunk and 70 merchant mariners lost their lives. The *Rose Castle,* a Canadian Merchant Navy steamer was attacked , with a loss of 28 Merchant Navy men. Among them were 5 Newfoundlanders. Members of the Newfoundland Militia Regimental Home Guard (of which my father was one), were also stationed in Bell Island, to guard its defensive fortress and gun formations . On December 12, 1942, the Knights of Columbus Hostel, a centre for military of all stripes, was putting off a dance when the place went up, in what accounts attribute to some sort of explosion, planned and executed by German saboteurs. 99 people died.

A morbid question played itself around in John Mahoney's head as he pored over his findings: where were the bodies, or in some horrific cases, parts of bodies, of all these unfortunate military men taken temporarily, following their tragic deaths? It's not likely Bell Island had a morgue. Some victims of the Knights of Columbus Fire, the city morgue being full, were laid out temporarily at the Catholic Cadet Corps Armory and the Church Lads Brigade Armory which were hastily put into service as emergency morgues.   The victims of the torpedoed ships must have been taken somewhere, temporarily, but where. He knew that Fort Pepperrell had morgue facilities, and the Canadian Navy more than likely brought their victims to Halifax. Could it be that some of them were taken to the morgue that now housed his workplace for so many years? Could the soldier ghost be one of those poor tragic men, in a limbo time zone, not really realizing he was dead, trying to cross over, to find a resting place for his wandering soul? And could the other military dressed apparitions others had seen at the production plant be ghosts of those placed in that morgue as well?   To pin down his details further of the clothes the soldier ghost was wearing,

John did some research of old military photos of Canadian and Newfoundland military men of both world wars. He found some that made his heart beat faster. The uniform that most closely resembled that which he had witnessed on the soldier ghost was that of a member of the Newfoundland Militia. John perused the library and found what he could on the details of the Newfoundland Militia/Regiment and Home Guard during World War Two. While reading, his hair stood on end. The Newfoundland Militia members, among their duties, often had to guard the inmates at the internment camp in Pleasantville. When the inmates were enjoying their recreation hour, and swimming in Quidi Vidi Lake, they were called back to shore by a long and pronounced whistle, executed by the attending soldier guard who wore a whistle around his neck. The soldier who had appeared to John repeatedly had a quite visible whistle hanging down his chest!

Could one of these soldier guards be his soldier ghost? Quidi Vidi Lake is directly across from the production plant facility, which was then a morgue. Other theories came into play. The soldier ghost could be a drowning victim, or an accident victim, or a victim of foul play.   He could be one of any number of Newfoundland, Canadian or American soldiers who sailed to Bell Island on leave time, ostensibly to relax and date girls who lived there. They could have met with some sort of fatal misfortune or accident. Even though the uniform on his soldier ghost most closely resembled that of the Newfoundland Militia, who had their headquarters at Shamrock Field and Lester's Field in St. John's. The scenarios were getting too close for comfort. John had no desire to look further. His cool and collected brain was starting to take a beating. His research had gained him some insight, and a sense of relief, but he was going to stop there.   He determined to dwell no more on the soldier ghost, and got on with his life and job. Some time passed. If his workmates had seen or heard things, they kept it to themselves. He hoped whomever was haunting his workplace had finally found peace at last.

March Of The Metal Plates (The Grand Finale)

In the winter of 2018, John was working night shift, repairing motors in a section of the plant which acted as a drainage for certain byproducts of the facility. It was around 3 A.M., and the place was empty, except for a Commissionaire who was located about 4 minutes walk away, through several hallways , corridors, and heavy steel doors. Large   metal plates covered the drainage areas, to prevent anyone walking on them to step down haplessly. If people were present in the area and walking over the drainage section, the sound of the protective metal plates clanking could be loudly heard. As well, the people walking would be in full view, and fully detectable on security cameras.   John was busy at his repairs when he suddenly heard the loud clanking of the metal plates, signifying someone was walking over them. He looked. No one was there. He went back to his work. Fifteen minutes later, the unmistakeable sounds of heavy feet walking on the metal plates reverberated again. He again looked. No one there.   The metal clanking kept repeating, the booming sounds of many feet wearing heavy footwear marching through the area, unseen. John decided to walk the 4-minute walk to the Commissionaire's station.

"Is anything showing?" He asked. "I'm hearing definite sounds of footsteps on the plates but can't see anyone." The Commissionaire checked his screen and scanned the sophisticated, high definition cameras overhead. "No. There is no one here John." John went back, mystified and feeling increasingly more uncomfortable as he resumed his work. About ten minutes later, again the loud stomping of heavy feet on the metal plates over the drainage area resounded again. No one was there. This time John lost his patience. He once more trudged the by now wearying walk to the Commissionaire's station, cursing himself that he had forgotten his cell phone outside.   "Is someone trying to have some mischief around here tonight? There's footsteps on the metal plates, but no one is there that I can see."   The Commissionaire,   seeing his frustration, once again did a sweep of overhead and all around.   He scrutinized the screen for a good long time. "I'm telling you, John, there is no one around here. We are the only ones here."

   And so it goes on. It seems that the restless soldier ghosts, and all the ghosts of Pleasantville, will never be at peace.

THE SINGING GHOST OF GOLDEN BAY

Golden Bay on the Avalon Peninsula's south- east coast is a very isolated area, with high cliffs and precipice no human could ever venture on. As far as anyone knew, no one had ever lived there. Maybe a scattered sheep could pick its wobbly way over the narrow cliff edges which tower dangerously down over the ragged cliffs to the sea. The remoteness, and stunning, rugged beauty along with the stark loneliness of the place drew two brothers, Harry and Ernest Fewer, who had a thirst to explore, and dare the eerie silence. On a clear day in August, 2011, they set off to do just that, landing on the ironically smooth and white-sanded beach in their motorboat. They hiked and climbed until they reached a treacherous high ledge, and crept stealthily forward. Not a sound could be heard. Not even a bird singing or a bee buzzing. No living being at all seemed to exist here, of any species. The two hikers stood drinking it all in, catching their breath and getting their cameras ready. Suddenly, they heard a voice. It was the voice of a woman, humming and singing. There was not a soul in sight anywhere. It was not humanly possible for anyone to be below, among the craggy cliff spires, and thunderous breakers crashing against the rocks jutting out.

They looked all around. The view was clear: a beautiful calm, sunny day, with the exception of the breakers below from the wild seas which boomed like cannon going off, thousands of feet down from the mountainous cliffs. The singing and humming continued. "Did you hear that?" Harry asked Ernest. "Err...hear what?" said Ernest, a little pale-faced.

 "The singing. A woman singing."

  "Yes. I thought I was imagining it. I was wondering if you heard it." They stopped, stood still, and listened even more intently. No mistaking it, it was a clear woman's voice humming away , in seemingly quiet contentment. And it was coming from very near , as if she were standing right next to them. Harry was sure he could feel her breath. At the same time, the unmistakeable scent of freshly baking bread wafted through the air.   No more was said. The brave explorers who were not so brave anymore retraced their steps back over the dangerously narrow precipice, and walked swiftly across the beautifully lonely barren grassland to the boat, each silently glad they had made it safely. They never went to Golden Bay again, only too happy to leave the singing housewife humming her tunes and baking her bread from the centuries-old recesses of the beyond.

THE HARD-WORKING CHEF OF AN EAST END INN

A busy Inn in St. John's , in operation for decades, and situated close to the international airport, caters to a wide and copious diversity of people. As in such a facility, chefs are well-trained and dedicated.   Doug Wall was such a chef, affable, and meticulous in his food preparation and serving. However , as in his work, in his play he possessed the same ebullience ; he enjoyed himself to the fullest. Friends and co-workers could always rely on Doug to be the life of the party at staff functions, and more than once his embarrassed wife would leave the celebrations, mortified at her husband's imbibing of too much spirits. Nonetheless, he was a popular, easygoing, well-liked fellow who unfortunately passed away about twenty years ago. Over those years, desk workers and night clerks at the Inn doing their nightly rounds began to hear spooky stories of strange sightings and sounds in the kitchen at night, when the cooking machinery was turned off and the place was closed. These new workers had never met or known Doug Wall, given it had been over two decades since he had worked there.

One night auditor in particular, Darryl Moore, on patrol one night, was shocked to see, when passing the darkened, locked kitchen, the full body apparition of a man, dressed in chef's uniform of a white coat, trousers and high hat, busily clanging away with his pots and pans. At first Darryl thought new things were happening with the hotel, that the kitchen was now operating at night again. "He was so real," Darryl explained. "Just as I am talking to you now; he was a real live person. I could see his face, his features, the colour of his hair under the hat. I could see his gold watch shining, and he was also wearing a gold chain. But the rest of the restaurant was dark, no people there, no activity, and the only light was the eerie shadows around the guy. It was then I knew this was a phantom, a ghost, and the hair stood up on my head. I got out of there real fast, although my knees felt pretty weak, and I couldn't concentrate too well the rest of the night." The apparition stuck in Darryl's head, until a chance coffee with a group of recently met friends seemed to solve the identity of the energetic chef from the other realm.

The friends were chatting casually, until one of them mentioned he had worked at this Inn over twenty years ago. Darryl, trying to sound as subtle as he could, asked him who the chefs were at that time. The friend said, "Well, a lot of them came and went, you know, but there was one, a really friendly one, who stayed a long time, a hard worker and good at his job. Only thing is, he liked to drink a lot on weekends. " The friend smiled.

"Always up for a good time Doug was, and a bit flashy, always wore gold chains and watches. He died suddenly about twenty years ago. Darryl swallowed. "Did he have light hair and about six feet tall ?" The friend looked at Darryl, animated. "Why yes he did. Did you know him?"

"No," Darryl answered. "But I saw a picture of him among the staff photo albums." It was a white lie, but Darryl couldn't come right out and say he had seen the ghost of Doug Wall. The pleasant, popular chef who liked his guests so much he is still serving them from beyond after twenty years.

The Used Car Ghost

Urban legends abound with accounts of car ghosts. They remain a well of fascination for most, and almost everyone has a creepy one to tell, whether real or imagined. But when a creepy experience comes from not only a rational, intelligent, conscientious man, but also several members of his friends and family, one starts to think that maybe it's true. Add to that the capture of the troublesome phenomenon on a camera or phone, and it's air tight.

Dave Knight lived in St. John's with his wife and family of 3 sons and a daughter. His oldest son, Kevin, was in the market for a good used car, and after a goodly number of trips to the car lots, found one , a Chevy Impala, at a reputable used car lot. He stored it in his father's garage, while he was out of the province working for a few months. His father, Dave, a retired engineer with time on his hands, loved to tinker with quality used cars, and every day he would visit the garage, and vacuum, sweep and polish the car to perfection. Sometimes he would take it out for a short run. By the time it was close to the day Kevin was coming home, Dave was satisfied the car was mechanically and aesthetically in tip-top shape.

The day before Kevin was to fly home, Dave went out to the garage as usual, to get the lawnmower to do some cutting. As he passed Kevin's car, gleaming from the wax job he had refined the day before, he smiled. The smile froze on his face, as a man was sitting in the car, his hands on the steering wheel. Dave moved closer, until he was an inch from the driver's window. His first impulse was to open the car door and demand to know who the man was. And how did he get there! The car doors had been locked, and he had installed a security alarm on the garage door only a few weeks ago. He was dealing with a break-in, and attempted robbery by the looks of things. He hesitated. The intruder could be armed. But he did think it strange that the stranger didn't move his head, and his face had a pasty tinge. As he stood wondering what to do, apprehensive and frustrated, staring at the man who was staring straight ahead wearing a cap and sunglasses, all of a sudden there was nothing. The man was gone. He had just disappeared. Cold shivers passed through Dave, and finally he opened the locked doors, and looked inside. Everything looked the same as he had left it.   "I felt weird," he says. "Real weird. He was real, but I couldn't help doubting myself. It was kind of a hot day and I had been working hard. Could I have imagined it?"

 He decided not to mention the strange occurrence, and Kevin came home. He continued to store the car in his father's garage, not really needing it on a daily basis and he lacked the room at his own place. One day, a week later, he walked in his father's house looking pale. "There was a man in the car," he said. "He was just sitting there. Then he was gone." Father and son commiserated over the vision they had seen. They decided that if one of them saw the apparition again, they would take a photo with their cell phone, to prove to each other and themselves their own credibility. However, they were not to mention the sightings to the rest of the family. Sure enough, about two weeks later, Dave, whose nerves were a little strung by this point, saw the man again as he walked in the garage. He was the same as before, sitting intently with his hands on the steering wheel, a ball cap on his head, and wearing sunglasses. Whipping out his phone, Dave took a photo, seconds before the man evaporated once more into nothingness. The image was clear and detailed. Dave couldn't sleep properly for nights, and worried about Kevin, who had seen it as well. He hoped that was the end of it, and tried to keep his wife Joy from going in the garage at all. But it was summer, and she was working at flower plantings. One day while Dave was gone to the Mall, she went in the garage to get some potting soil. As she passed by Kevin's car she saw the ghostly mystery man, sitting up , with his hands on the steering wheel. Not realising first who it was, she thought it was a friend or neighbour and approached him. He disappeared into nothingness before her shocked gaze. When Dave came back, Joy was almost in hysterics, never having witnessed such before. He decided to come clean with her.   "By this time we were all afraid to drive the car. Kevin would not get in it," Dave said. "For that matter, we were nervous about even going in the garage. All of us, my sons, my daughter, my wife, me, all saw this guy. We wanted it to stop, and we felt foolish telling anybody. ."

 Finally, one of the other sons, Ned, who was not as freaked out, decided to try and find out who the ghostly car jacker was.   He
went to the root, the car dealership on Kenmount Road,   and demanded to know the previous owners of the Chev Impala . There had been only one, a taxi company. Ned tracked down the taxi company, on Ropewalk Lane, and without preamble walked in and showed the manager the photo of the resident ghost. He didn't say when or where it was taken. The lie that he felt was the only route came next. "This is a friend of mine from long ago, " he said.   "I've been wanting to reconnect with him. Someone at the pub next door said he worked here for awhile."   The taxi company manager scrutinized the photo on Ned's cell phone. He looked at him. "So you knew Sam did you? He was with us a long while. Sad to say he   died a few months ago, and we sold his taxi. He only drove the one taxi, in fact was

bar

33

quite devoted to it. It was a Chev Impala." Ned said thanks, grateful for the information, and bolted out the door. At his father's house he made one simple suggestion. "You'd better get rid of that car." He said. "I really don't think any of us will know peace with that around." The car was duly put in the classifieds for a bargain price. "I felt guilty about selling it to anyone," Dave said. "But hopefully it will be okay. Maybe he had a problem at this place for some reason. Maybe he didn't like all that cleaning and shining and tinkering. Or maybe he couldn't bear to leave his taxi behind. Some guys are pretty weird about their cars. I'm just glad the whole thing has been solved. I'll never forget it, it was a very unsettling experience for me and my family."

STRANGER IN THE GRAVEYARD

Tim's Story:

I go to visit my parents' plot at Christmas, Mothers' Day and Fathers' Day. They are interned together at Holy Sepulchre Cemetery, Topsail Road, St. John's . Last Mothers' Day I had a really strange experience there. I tried to rationalize it as a trick of the sun or something, but it really was weird, I guess is the right word. I had gotten up earlier than usual, and figured I may as well get an early start on my visit to my parents' grave, as I was doing things with the wife and kids later. It was a Sunday, and at that hour, around 7:30, it was relatively quiet around the city. It was a lovely, sunny morning. I had bought flowers the day before, and after a coffee at Tim Horton's I set out. I was bending over the headstones, just quietly thinking about them both . I had often wished I could have had many more years with them, and it was probably around these lines I was thinking , when I heard a man's voice right behind me. He must have been a tall man, since the voice seemed to come from a distance up. It was friendly, hale and hearty, but it intruded on my thoughts, and I really didn't want to engage in a conversation with him. "You know what?" The voice said in a rather large, cheerful way. "If everyone here stood up today we would have some crowd of people! And that's a fact!" I looked up from my bending position and saw a man, looking to be in his fifties, tall, wearing a dark suit , white shirt and tie. He was pleasant looking. I turned back, rather startled, and was about to answer him, although I was thinking what a rude thing to do, interrupt someone who was visiting a loved one's gravesite, when , on turning my head to look up, he was gone. In a flash. The graveyard was deserted, and the section I was on being on flat terrain with no trees, I had a full view of anyone coming and going from all directions. He was nowhere to be seen.   I told myself I had to be making a mistake, he had to be somewhere, but no, he had disappeared.   I started to sweat a little, but got control and remembered something my mother used to say, "it was just a poor soul needing a prayer." So I blessed myself and said an extra prayer for the collective souls in that graveyard that day.

SHE DIDN'T LIKE ME

Doreen's Story:

I live in an apartment building in St. John's. I won't reveal what section of the city, but it is a decent building with decent tenants. I have never believed in ghosts, and am not a nervous person given to flights of fancy. My apartment is a two-bedroom, and I use one bedroom for a computer room . I spend a good deal of time on the computer, since I work from home. About two years ago, things started happening which I laughed off, but could be connected to some kind of paranormal activity, I really don't know. I do know they seemed rather strange. The first incident was my brand new flat screen 30-inch T.V. shutting off for no apparent reason while I would be watching something interesting. I didn't think anything of it at all, assuming it was a cable issue, and really didn't care as long as it came back on and I was able to finish watching my shows. One weekend I had a visitor, and the T.V. started acting up again. My visitor, whom I'll call Dorothy, was a little bothered, which surprised me, since ghosts and paranormal stuff had never entered my mind. Following that, a lamp kept blinking in and out, which I also had a rational explanation for: faulty wire. I threw out the lamp. The following week the matching lamp began blinking in and out, and out that went in the trash as well. Then the chandelier in my kitchen/dinette started going off in the middle of a meal. I replaced the small bulbs, and it kept happening. By this time I was fed up enough to call the company maintenance to check my fuse box, and other electrical stuff, just to be on the safe side. Everything was okay. Then one night at about 3 A.M. I was awakened suddenly by my old Hewlett Packard printer going loudly....rat...tat...rat...rat...tat...tat, working away, although I was sure I had turned it off and unplugged the whole power bar which I had a habit of doing every night. I rolled over and went back to sleep, not perturbed at all. Perhaps a loose connection somewhere I told myself. One night I was in my computer room at about 2, rushing to finish a job, when all of a sudden a deep chill and trembling went right through me. I had the most horrible and pronounced FEAR for no reason, and I had never been so cold. It felt as if something or someone had gone right in through my body and come out again. I had never experienced anything like it. A few weeks later my printer started coming on again, all by itself, rat...tat...tat...rat..tat..tat with no paper in it after the whole computer/printer system had been turned off, and the power bar unplugged. It kept on going for about 20 minutes, printing out an invisible document with no paper in it. I went and stood at the computer room door, and this time I felt a bit shaky as I could see no lights lit up, but the printer was going mad, again with no paper in it. I was scared to go any further. This continued off and on for months, waking me from sleep, occurring at intervals of two or three weeks. One day a light bulb went off in my head, and I wondered why I hadn't thought of it before, but, as I mentioned, I don't believe in ghosts. An older lady, Mrs.

Maddison, in an apartment next to me, had died about six months before. I didn't know her very well, she kept to herself, and I had no idea she had been ill. She had a dog who was a real yapper, and sometimes I would step in the dog's droppings outside, in the well-kept little grass plots reserved for sitting on a nice evening. Clearly she wasn't using a pooper scoop, and this used to irritate me. Her door was inches from mine, and one night not too long before she died, the dog was going mad barking. I had an early appointment the next day, and got virtually no sleep. I politely mentioned it to her, and she fixed me with a very hostile gaze, saying a few choice words. Could there be a connection I wondered. She had never really liked me; she knew I had a problem with the barking and the droppings.

However, I was shocked when she passed away, and under my breath one night I whispered, "I'm sorry, Mrs. Maddison. I didn't know you had been ill. I hope you rest in peace." I don't know if my words had an effect, but oddly enough, after I had toyed with this scenario in my mind, the strange activity stopped, and did not happen again.

LET THERE BE LIGHT...AND LIGHT...AND LIGHT

GLENDA'S STORY:

My husband and I were at the Blueberry Festival in Brigus some years ago. We decided to stay overnight, and next day went looking around . We noticed a roadside sale that looked interesting. We stopped and got out to look . I spotted a large light fixture with the tulip-shaped encasings. This one was six-pronged , and gold/brown in colour. We weren't quite sure if it would work or not when installed, but took a chance, since it was so 1970's, and I loved it. We were going to get new bulbs, but the bulbs were already in it, so we decided to use them for as long as they worked. When we got home we decided to install the light fixture in the rec room downstairs. He found the cords and connected them up to the wires in the fixture. The

fixture worked perfectly, each bulb seemed to be brand new. We were
expecting the bulbs to go at any time, since they were the old-fashioned
kind, not the long - burning ones which are in style now. But they kept on
working, the same bulbs, week after week, month after month. All the rest
of the bulbs in the house we had to replace every couple of months, but not
those in that fixture. They just kept working, and not only working, but the
longer they were on, the brighter seemed the light coming from them. One
day I said to my husband, "Do you know its been two years since we bought
that fixture?" He looked surprised and shook his head. Life went on, and
we had more important things to think about than the old-fashioned 70's
fixture down in the rec room. It wasn't that the rec room was used less than
the rest of the house; our teenagers practically lived down there and like all
teenagers, didn't spare on lights, blasting them all the time. The bulbs kept
burning, inside those old tulip-shaped encasings, with no signs of giving out.
Three years passed. Four. Five. We went through numerous light bulbs in
that time, but not the ones in that old 70's tulip light fixture we had bought
in Brigus years ago. Finally, one night as we were sitting in the rec room, I
looked at the brightly burning bulbs in that fixture and suddenly I got a
funny feeling. It had been SIX YEARS, and those old-fashioned bulbs in that
decades old fixture were still glowing, and to me, with an unnatural glow.
I turned off the switch and let them cool . Then I told my husband to
remove those old bulbs and put in new ones. "Why?" He asked.   "It's time
for them to go," I said. He did as I asked, and put in new bulbs. After a few
days, I noticed they were brighter than the other bulbs in the house that
were the same wattage. Call me crazy, but I told my husband to go get his
tool belt and take out that old 70's tulip light fixture from the ceiling and
throw it in the garbage. He asked why. I said I just got sick of looking at it, it
was just a big old thing. He wanted to keep the light bulbs he had just
bought, saying they were still good, but when his back was turned, out they
went in the garbage as well.   Now , whenever we need a new light fixture,
out to Kents or Home Hardware we go. I will never buy a light fixture from

a roadside sale again. Whoever was in it didn't want to leave.

TRUE STORIES TOLD BY GABRIEL RYAN:

As mentioned in the introduction to this book, Gabriel Ryan was my father. He was born on April 15, 1921, in St. Joseph's, St. Mary's Bay, heart of the Irish Loop . He spent his childhood like all the rest of the children in this small outport settlement: going to a two-room school, helping his father in the woods, and playing in the then village's grassy roads and meadows. There were no cars when Gabriel was growing up, no electricity, and no "outsiders" to mar the peace, quiet, and innocence of their rural life. Gabriel grew up spending the long summer evenings on a grassy bank listening to someone's visiting uncle tell old yarns, or sitting fascinated in the lamplight on a stormy winter's evening, as his grandfather told him tales of sea and land while the fire crackled in the old woodstove. Into this fertile setting "ghosts" were a natural belief, and events and happenings of a supernatural nature were related to spellbound listeners, and believed to be true. As a boy, Gabriel worked as an apprentice to the stern, crusty old Irish priest, Father John Enright, who would threaten to turn them all into goats if they didn't behave! The simplicity and influences of those days was a vehicle for many of his stories in later life, when he became a father and had children to sit wide-eyed in another kitchen across the meadow from his born home, with woodfire and lamplight and visiting neighbours, little having changed in social amenities in the community since he was a boy. I and my four siblings were lucky enough to have been raised in this kitchen, in such a rich setting!

The Ghost Of Mickey Quinn

According to Gabriel Ryan, who was born and grew up in St. Mary's Bay, ghost stories were as common as having your tea and toutons every day. With gravel roads, narrow at that, between communities, people often came home white-faced, saying they saw ghosts here and saw ghosts there. The following is one of Gabriel's true stories of a tragedy on a lonely wintry road, and the snow-covered phantom who can't find peace:

Mickey Quinn was one of many hard-working men without cars who lived in one of the small communities , Riverhead. He often walked between communities, a distance of 10-18 miles. A rough feat in any weather, but in winter, only for the very hardy. But for the hardiest of them all, which Mickey was, the merciless elements finally did him in.

The road between the communities of Riverhead and St. Joseph's was especially narrow, and the marshy flats on the sides a popular area for setting rabbit snares. One morning, having set their snares some days previously, Jerome Ryan, Gabriel's father, and the police constable who was stationed there at the time left to go in this road to "haul" the snares. They were about two miles from St. Joseph's. It was just after daylight , a clear and warm early summer day. After they had walked about two miles, they saw a man approaching them. He was dressed in heavy winter clothes, snow-covered, winter "Gators" (a term for boots), and wearing thick, homespun, knitted mitts which hung down long and soggy and were also snow-caked. The man had his head down, as though he were battling an unseen force. The constable , startled by the arctic-looking apparition on a clear warm day with no snow, asked Jerome who the man was. "Jerome, " he said. "Who's that man coming there?" Jerome answered, "Gar, boy, I don't know, there's a man coming out there all right." They kept on walking, and in a few seconds they looked again, and Jerome exclaimed, "that man is gone!" There was really nowhere for the man to go, there being only a little tree tuck on each side of the road; everything else was a flat, clear, marshy place with clear visibility. They looked through the little tree tuck and all around. No one could be seen from a good distance away.

"God," the constable said, "he's not there." He was bewildered . They went on walking. They had to go in about another mile or so to haul the rabbit snares . Jerome had to go to one side of the road to look at his, and the constable had to go to the other side of the road, to look at his. They parted. They were no sooner gone than they were back to the road again. The constable was clearly affected by the disappearing human snowman and wouldn't move another inch by himself. "Boy I can't go."

"Boy I can't go either constable." Jerome said. The two of them were forced to go together, and do one, and then the other's snares. The wintery traveller was a well-known sight by travellers of that road for many years. His name was Michael ("Mickey") Quinn, and he had died on that same road, in a snowstorm in the winter. He was found dead in there, and had appeared to many , as he was the night he died, bucking his head against the blizzard winds. "This was supposed to be him, the ghost, coming and vanished clear of him you know," says Gabriel Ryan. "He was wearing the long mitts hanging down and everything and this was a summer's day. He's buried in the cemetery up home in St. Joseph's, being found dead in there in the winter, travelling this lonely road, and a snowstorm came on and he couldn't make it."

Mickey Quinn didn't just roam the roads without a purpose in mind. He watched for cars too, and often got lifts from people who saw him walking ahead, and stopped to pick him up. It was only afterwards that they would discover to their horror they had been transporting a ghost. Dr. McGrath was a physician who, stationed in St. Mary's, serviced communities all over St. Mary's Bay, where he held clinics in people's living rooms and such. In the winter time, young boys would be dispatched to shovel the roads, to help get the good doctor's car on the road to a call. One day he got a call to St. Joseph's, and was on his way back to St. Mary's when he saw a man walking ahead of him. It was the same area as the others who had offered to help, and who had the same experience. The man walking ahead of him had long mitts hanging down, and looked bedraggled, as if he had been walking for some time. The doctor stopped to pick the man up, to give him a lift. He opened the door, and no one came. He got out and looked around and no one was there. So he got back in the car, and started it up again. He could feel a weight in the seat next to him, and the seat squeaking and sagging, as if someone had stepped inside and sat down. He could feel the seat next to him dragging down with this weight until he got as far as Riverhead. Then he heard the sound of the passenger door opening, and the weight was lifted from the seat.   He knew then it was the ghost of someone needing a ride, and that someone was Mickey Quinn's ghost who hadn't been ready to leave the world until a terrible storm claimed his unwilling life.

 In the hilltop pathway up to the site of the old church in St. Joseph's, there is a flat headstone, beaten and battered by winds from the sea, and grown over with weeds. The headstone is not in the populated area of the cemetery, but directly on the walkway. Scurrying and heedless feet have trodded over it for many decades, on their way to mass, benediction, weddings, funerals, baptisms, first communion, confirmation, and the like. The engraved letters are barely legible, but still decipherable. The marking on the headstone reads "Sacred to the memory of Michael Quinn, lost in storm." The year is illegible, but local legend attests to it being sometime in the early 1900's. The headstone is as forgotten and lonely as his lonely, tragic death on the stormy road so many years ago.

Poor Malachy Needs A Prayer

Gabriel Ryan told a chilling story of a priest he worked for as a young boy, Father John Enright, in the rural community of St. Joseph's. He worked for him for 4 years, starting at 14. Some of them were creepy times. The Irish priest had a peculiar penchant for holding funerals at midnight. The communities in St. Mary's Bay in those years, the 1930's, were creepy enough as it was, at night, with no electric lights, only kerosene oil lamps in homes, and battery flashlights to light their way when walking on roads as black as pitch. Add to that the bells in the Belfry which Gabriel had to toll during the midnight service when someone died, to announce their solemn passing, and we have a scene straight out of Brod Stoker.

Once, on a calm fall night, after dark, following the burial of a man named Malachy McKnight, not his real name,   Gabriel was in the scullery washing his hands and cleaning up after milking the cows, when he heard the housekeeper say to the priest, "Father, there's something out making a noise in back of the house."

" Wisht," He said in his Irish brogue. "Tis your imagination."

The housekeeper would not be mollified. "No, Father, there's something out there, a noise." He ignored her, and went on in his study. The housekeeper kept hearing the noise, and pestered him again with more pleas.

"There's something out there, a noise." She repeated.

"Ah," he said, "I'll go out anyway to satisfy ye." Gabriel saw him passing out through the corridor to go out through the door with his prayerbook in his hand. He was gone about five minutes and came in and closed the door. "You won't hear it any more," he said. "That was poor Malachy, he was in a little trouble. (Malachy was the man who was buried a few hours before). "He's okay now," he said. "He had a little trouble, he came back to see me." The "trouble" of course, meaning he was having difficulty crossing over to the other side, after leaving this earth only a few hours before. In Irish and Celtic lore, the confused spirit of the deceased person requires the prayers and supplications of a religious entity to guide him along his journey to the afterlife.

THE MAN ON THE ROCK: WHAT THE POLICE OFFICER SAW

This true story was passed down from my maternal grandfather, Sergeant James B. Power

In the 1930's in small towns outside of St. John's, policing services were provided by one Constable from the Royal Newfoundland Constabulary. This officer usually lived where the courthouse, magistrates and official offices were located, and served several communities by travelling when needed by car. When the need arose for more pressing court matters, he travelled to the Newfoundland Supreme Courthouse located in St. John's. Sergeant James B. Power was one of those police officers serving the communities of Harbour Main, Avondale, Conception Harbour, and points in between during those years. He resided in Harbour Main with his wife Mary and several small children. He had a car, but often liked to walk to his duties in fair weather, as the little towns were located within a distance of two or three miles from each other.

Sgt. Power was an intelligent, rational, and well-read man, and a good and fair police officer . He had been a foreign-going sea captain and served overseas in WW1 . He had experienced much in his travels, and met people from many cultures . He sustained a bayonet in the side in the Battle of Beaumont Hamel, but came back from the war ready to put it behind him and carry on with a life which included marriage, a career, and children. He considered himself a logical and level-headed person, and did not entertain the notion of ghosts or anything of a paranormal nature. Nevertheless, on one night in the fall in the 1930's, he had reason to question the existence of both, when he had been coming home from police duty at a dance in the hall in Conception Harbour. The dances were sometimes   a rowdy and boisterous , often troublesome time due to drinking, and the possible presence of moonshine which lurked in those years in this town and surrounding areas.

It was a beautiful October night, just the kind of night James enjoyed . The air was crisp and there was a full harvest moon, which bathed everything in a light clear as day. He was relieved his shift was over. The parish hall in Conception Harbour had been packed, several fights had broken out, which he had to break up. He was enjoying the peace and quiet of the pastoral country road, which happened to be bordered on one side by the town graveyard. After he had walked about fifteen minutes he was surprised to see , sitting on a large rock by the side of the road, a man. The man was sitting in a slumped position, his peaked cap down over his forehead, hiding his eyes. James assumed he was inebriated or sick, so he went over to see how he could help and get him home safely. "That looks like Paddy Mulligan," he thought. "One too many again." Paddy Mulligan was a Harbour Main native, a bachelor, who though harmless, was known for imbibing often of liquor, and moonshine if he could get it.

James walked over to the rock. "Hello there Paddy. Nice night we're having. What are you up to tonight? On the way home from the dance are you?" The man on the rock didn't answer; his head dropped further down, and his cap went further down , hiding his eyes even more. James walked closer. "It's getting late Paddy. Time to go home. Come on now, I'll help you up and you can walk along with me." Still no answer. The cap dropped to the man's nose. Three more times James attempted to garner an answer from the man he thought was Paddy Mulligan, but got none. His curious and stubborn behaviour finally started to get on James' nerves. "Now look here, Paddy. You have to get off that rock and come with me. I can't leave you here. You'll freeze to death. Come on now, that's a good man." Still nothing. The full moon shone down on the scene, on the man dressed in a suit coat and trousers, shirt and tie, slumped on the rock, with the peaked cap dropping ever further down over his face, as if he had fallen asleep. James started to lose his cool. "Damn it." He thought. "He's passing out on me."

"Now look here Paddy goddamnit," he said loudly. "Get up off that rock and come on with me!" James put out his night stick lightly to touch "Paddy's" shoulder to arouse him. The stick struck bare rock. The man was gone.

James stood there dumbfounded. He would not believe the evidence of his eyes. He had a large flashlight in his greatcoat pocket. He took it out and flashed it all around. No sign of Paddy, or the man he thought was Paddy. Due to the moonlight, he had a clear view of the flat pastures beyond bordered by rail fences. Not a soul was in sight. He crossed to the other side of the road and looked around, shining the flashlight in the scattered tree tuck, but he knew deep down that what he had seen wasn't of this world. Finally in frustration he struck the rock with his stick several more times, maybe as he told after, to conjure up the image again, to make some sense of it. *Who had he seen? What had he seen?* He walked on home, pondering. Try as he could to not believe he had seen a spirit, he was failing miserably, and with the sweat drops dropping off his nose and the knowledge that that graveyard was still not far behind him, he was glad to finally see his own light. His family were in bed. He hardly slept.

The next morning, Mary was surprised to see him lying on the sofa. Usually he would be alert and bright, dressed impeccably and off to his duties or his office papers. He had one question for her, "Do you want to go for a little drive?" Eschewing the walk, he and Mary drove in to Conception Harbour, and he stopped the car at the exact spot where he had the strange encounter. On the way he had told her the whole story. "I want to see that rock." He said. Together they stepped into the little clearing, to the exact location of the rock. There was no rock. Undisturbed leaves and dirt were in the spot where the large rock had been the night before. James shook his head. He turned the nightstick over and over in his hand. Mary had a strange look on her face. "How did you break the stick?" She suddenly asked. He looked at her, and in disbelief after turning the stick upside down could plainly see where pieces of splinter had come off the wooden stick, from where he had struck the rock in frustration the night before.

The Angry Ghost Of St. Patrick's Church

The cornerstone of St. Patrick's Roman Catholic Church in St. John's, Newfoundland was laid on September 17, 1855 by Bishop John T. Mullock, whose dream was to construct a cathedral in honour of the patron saint of Ireland, St. Patrick, and to build a church of equal par to the Basilica for the people of St. John's West. The laying of the cornerstone was attended also by distinguished clergy from Canada and the U.S. The church was designed in the late Gothic Revival, also termed Neo-Gothic style, by J.J. McCarthy, a prominent Irish architect. Following decades of stops and starts due to funds and materials, the church was completed and consecrated on August 28, 1881. It was designated a National Historic Site of Canada in 1990. In 1997 the Heritage Foundation of Newfoundland and Labrador declared St. Patrick's Church a Registered Heritage Structure. It is considered today one of the most beautiful and artful churches in all of North America.

However, with its century- plus age and history since its inception, it stands to ghostly reason there would be a spirit or two hanging around its hallowed steeples and walls.

   Linda Owens , not her real name, had a frightening experience with her camera, the night after she had been to a family wedding rehearsal at the church. Here is her story:

 My sister was getting married, and the family had appointed me as the unofficial wedding photographer, seeing I was always taking photos, and it would be more cost effective than hiring a professional portrait artist. I was only too happy, since my camera and I are pretty well joined at the hip.

I love old churches. Newfoundland has many. I love the beauty, history and architecture. However, I am rather embarrassed to say I had not been in St. Patrick's Church prior to my sister's wedding rehearsal. They were married there in 2010. As soon as I was inside the church the evening of the rehearsal I was struck by the wonder of the place. I had already driven around it at various times, and taken outdoor pictures, even snapping the neon green statue of St. Patrick which stood outside one night. The evening of the rehearsal, while things were being set up and the wedding party were waiting for the full crew to arrive, I wandered around inside with my camera, snapping as discreetly as I could the statues and artful things I saw. I was captivated by the place. While the rehearsal was in full swing, I captured photos of the wedding party as they bantered with each other, and also photos of the prepared-for ceremony. It was a joyous time on a beautiful summer night, a time to relax before the stress of the big event. We all came back to my place after, to partake of a special spread I had prepared.

   The wedding was two days away. On the eve of the wedding, I was idly sitting at my laptop, and decided to upload the photos of the rehearsal I had taken at St. Patrick's Church to my computer.   I was curious to see how they came out. I loved the interior photos of the statues, etc. I then came to those I had taken of the wedding party all lined up by the altar where the priest and organist and all the other officiates were giving instructions. I glanced casually at everyone in the photos, and was pleased at how it all looked, envisioning my sister in her wedding dress, and her handsome groom by her side. As I was going down the row of people in the pictures, my breath caught in my throat. What a shock and a fright! There was a woman, maybe in her 60's or 70's , who was standing among the wedding party. She had grey curly hair, wore a loud, long dress, clunky, 70's looking glasses, and wearing the most hateful, most evil expression I had ever seen in my life. Her mouth was turned up in a grimace as ugly and horrible as hell itself, as she glared at the scene with open hostility and hate. And she was standing with the wedding party! Oh My God I thought. Who is she! I felt weak with the horror of it, to see such a spectre among my lovely family in their wedding rehearsal at St. Patrick's Church. I knew it wasn't a real person. I knew well each and every one of the wedding party, and she surely wasn't one of them! She was on every one of the wedding party images, and over her shoulder and hovering her ugly countenance there was a greyish tinge. It is a trick of the camera, I thought , it has to be, but I was so horrified by it my chest got tight and cold shivers were going through me. I was home alone, my husband was working evening shift. I felt silly calling him , about such a trivial thing as photos on a memory card, but I did anyway. It was just freaking me out, and the wedding was the next day. I was Maid of Honor, and I wanted to get my rest and sleep that night. I explained it to him, and he said not to worry, don't be silly, the usual stuff; it was a double exposure, batteries flashing before they finally go, images clashing with each other; get off the computer and make a nice cup of tea, the wedding is tomorrow, etc. etc. I did as he told me.

About two weeks later, the wedding excitement behind, I showed a good friend who was in the wedding party the photos, asking her if she had ever seen or known the ugly woman. She did not. Over lunch a few of us discussed, even laughed about it, and one friend said she had heard about an old woman decades back, who, upset at her daughter marrying a foreign man, had screamed out in church and dropped dead. I took that as one of many strange city stories which maybe had no basis in fact. But it did give me the creeps, and in spite of myself, I wondered what if. Later, I realized that more than likely, it was a trick of the camera, but it made me wonder at the souls of all the people who had their funerals in that old church, and all the people who had attended that ancient artifice over the centuries and who were now long dead. Do they feel invaded and violated by the outside world, especially in the digital age. Do they sometimes feel like exacting revenge? Food for thought for anyone taking photos inside these old stone bastions. I don't think I'll be doing it again, even though more than likely it was a trick of the camera or a double exposure. We'll say it was anyway. But Like the saying in show biz....the camera doesn't lie.

THE CURSE OF Thomas Mackey

This true story is the original account of the vagaries of a family friend, Thomas Mackey, (not his real name), who was terrorized and afflicted with a horrible curse in his youth. He was afflicted following his blocking a pathway in a fishing ground haunted by the angry, restless spirits of a tragic shipwreck. It is the genesis of my popular published novel, Hannigan's Hand.

Thomas Mackey, not his real name, was born and raised in a town on the southeast coast of the Avalon Peninsula. He lived in a quaint , almost storybook house in a long lane bordered by rail fences and wild rosebushes, in pastoral meadowland and barns and outbuildings he tended with loving care. Following the passing of his parents, he and his brother stayed on in the house, fishing, farming, and in the case of Thomas, a stint in the army and working at the Gander Air Force Base his sole forays from his beloved abode. He was a friendly, easygoing type of person, well-liked by all who knew him.

As a young man, Thomas would often go on fishing trips with his uncles, father and neighbours and friends. These trips which involved sometimes weeks at a time would take place in often remote places, and necessitated the setting up of camps, akin to a work camp which sheltered them and had to be supplied with the basic elements of survival, which included keeping a steady supply of wood on hand at all times.   And it's around this basic activity, wood gathering, that this increasingly horrific story revolves.

The parish priest in this specific town at that time, and for many years following, was Father John Enright. A full-blooded Irish cleric from the sod, he brought with him from Ireland the demonic superstitions and beliefs , including the curses of souls gone before, upon the unfortunate ones who dared defy the sacred spirits or disturb them in any way.   One of his repeated dire warnings to his flock was the mantra, "Never block a beaten path." This seemingly simple statement held a world of meaning, since it implied that those who had gone before, the souls of the departed who had trodden there, had first rights, in the event of sudden death or tragedy, where unfortunate people had died before their time. The remote coves around the coast of Newfoundland were for centuries the site of many shipwrecks, which involved deaths and drownings. The shipwrecks were sometimes accidental, other times designed, by criminal activity such as luring the ships to shore with false lights, so the livyers could steal the cargo. As Gabriel Ryan, who heard the story from the victim himself, stated, "there were many wrecks in those times, in that place , on that coast. Many boats went down, many people drowned."

One early fall day, somewhere around the early 1930's, plans were made for Thomas Mackey, his father and uncles, to make the trip to Broad Cove, a popular fishing ground in an isolated place on the southeast coast, for a fishing expedition. These expeditions were a necessity of the times, their families' lives depended on them, and certainly was not done for the purpose of fun or entertainment. They would be staying for a couple of weeks. A shipwreck involving a large vessel and the loss of many lives had happened there fairly recently, but if the fishing party had any prior knowledge of this occurrence, they chose not to let it bother them, and got on with the task in hand. Shortly after setting up camp, Thomas was given the task of chopping down some trees, sawing them up, and storing them in any available space, to use as firewood for the duration of their extended stay in the cove. Thomas took to the job with gusto, and by that evening, had stored up a healthy mound of wood in a pathway not far from the camps. By evening, he had finished the job, and feeling satisfied, made ready to retire for the night. Being a lovely calm evening, he decided to take a stroll on the beach, to get some fresh air, before turning in. As he walked, he noticed a figure some distance ahead. Thinking first it was one of his group, he was ready to shout a greeting, but quickly changed his mind upon noticing this man was large and stout, and clearly not anyone familiar he could recognize. As Thomas got closer, he almost passed out right there, for there before him was this huge man, or part of a man, approaching him, without a head. The headless man's clothes were in tatters, and green slime and bits of dead fish clung to what was left of the body. Thomas didn't know how he made it back to the camp, with the terrified state he was in. But this wasn't all he was forced to bear, as, attempting to enter the camp door, his left arm was grabbed forcefully by an unseen human grip. He couldn't get to clear it. Phantom human hands like giant claws were gripping his arm as in a vice grip. He called out weakly to his father and brother and the others, who were staying not all in one camp, but also in an adjoining one. They came running, as , in almost the same moment, the camp started to shake violently as in an earthquake.

"What's going on here?" His uncle shouted. "Everything is going mad!" The other occupants of the adjoining camp shouted back in unison. "Everything's going mad here too!" The violent shaking continued for another while, while outside it stayed calm and peaceful, with not a breath of wind nor a rock disturbed on the beach. Finally, it stopped, and the eldest man quietly suggested they all get down on their knees and say the Rosary. The next day, when Thomas awoke from a troubled and fitful sleep, his left hand and arm was swollen and fiery red. The eldest man, the leader of the expedition, ordered Thomas back home to be examined by the priest, or taken to hospital, since there was no roaming doctor available at the time. Father Enright , upon looking at what seemed to him to be a dangerous infection, told him he couldn't do anything with it, and for him to go out to the hospital in St. John's right away. At the hospital, it is not known what transpired, but another priest, who had his roots in that same bay, told him to go back to Father Enright, who, he said, "was the best doctor he could get." Father Enright, upon peering at the swollen arm and redness which was getting worse, proceeded to get a little lance, and lanced the arm, in an attempt to drain the infection, or whatever it was that was causing the arm to swell and take on the fiery red tinge.

"Oh," he said, in his thick Irish brogue, "dere it is and 'tis bad too." He lifted the damper from the stove where the fire was brightly burning, and threw the remnants of whatever he had lanced from the hand, a little black worm and some dirt and sticks, and which he had placed in a tissue, into the flames. "That's bad," he said. "That's it. Yeah, this is it, and it's bad too." He repeated.

"Now," He said to Thomas, "Go home and go to bed." He went down to see Thomas's mother and told her to close the drapes. "Put him in a dark room," he told her. "And if he wakes up don't be there when that breaks.

This is going to swell and break, and don't be in the room when it breaks."
Sometime during the next morning the infection or whatever it was broke,
and to quote Gabriel Ryan who told the story, "It broke, and whatever
came out of it went right across like a shot out of a gun ; it struck the
ceiling and everything, and then they called Father Enright again and he
said 'that's good. you're clear of it now. Oh that was a bad one. When did
you come to see it?'

Thomas told him the whole story, his piling the wood in the path, the
headless man, the gripping of his arm by unseen hands, the cabins shaking,
his waking with the swollen hand and arm. "Don't you ever block a beaten
path any more," Father Enright said. "Oh you'd better be careful in them
places, so many mariners, there's so many wrecks out there, and
everything. People drowned and everything . You know, there was no
control over vessels or nothing. They hit the rocks and they'd go ashore and
there was all kinds aboard o' them and everything. Anyway, don't ever
block a beaten path no more. Yeah, he was there. You were in his way and
that was it." Needless to say, Thomas had learned his lesson. As Gabriel
Ryan, a lifetime friend and recipient of the story from Thomas many times
put it, "Oh he had a hard time of it you know. Now this was true. He had a
hard time of it. He had like to lose his arm and everything."

THE STRANGE PREMONITION OF ELIZABETH RYAN

Tokens or premonitions are warnings and signals projected from unknown
entities in the spiritual and cosmic world, to portend danger or the
impending death of a loved one. These warnings can take the form of
fullbody sightings of the person doomed to die, or , other avenues such as
unexplainable happenings as simple as a burst of wind in a room, at the
very moment a loved one is in trouble. Such a sign came to Elizabeth Ryan
in her kitchen in St. Joseph's, St. Mary's Bay, on the night of December 12,

54

1942. The date was ominous. It was the night of the tragic Knights Of Columbus Fire, and two of Elizabeth's sons, Gabriel and Larry, members of the Newfoundland Militia, were stationed in St. John's on this night. They had attended the dance, and were in the building when the fire broke out.

Elizabeth Ryan, with her husband Jerome, were the parents of ten children. The family, like everyone in the community, were Catholic, and attended church on a regular basis. She was a lady of immeasurable faith. On this night she had found herself, in fact, praying. At home in St. Joseph's, she had been sitting with her knitting, listening to radio station VOCM, which had provided quickie features, chat, music, and news items to thousands of Newfoundlanders, connecting the island's communities together in a time before television. On this night, broadcasting from the Knights Of Columbus auditorium itself, Uncle Tim's Barn Dance Show provided an aural connection to her sons Gabriel and Larry, who were present in the audience.

Perhaps there had been a twinge of reception interference somewhere, for Elizabeth's big battery radio, at shortly after 11 P.M., began blasting static momentarily, then silence. She figured it was just that, some random technical problem, and decided to go to bed. As she crossed the dining room to her bedroom, however, she felt a burst of dreadfully cold air, "swooshing like a funnel, with a whistling sound, " sweep around her legs. The swishes of shooting air sped past her twice. Initially, to make concrete sense of it, she thought it may be the pet cat. However, the cat was nowhere to be found in the area. A palpable sense of dread filled her, and she was convinced that somehow, something very bad had happened to her two sons. She immediately fell to her knees and prayed, she would later recall, "the whole night through." Her night would grow long with worry and concern.

An older boy, Jim , a gunner in the artillery, was already seeing action in

Africa and Italy. Gabriel , age 21, was into his 3rd year with the Newfoundland Militia, and a Lance Corporal. Larry, his brother, had only just recently joined. On the night of December 12, 1942, they both had tickets to take in the barn dance at the hostel, which promised to be a fine time with the sale of over 400 tickets gone already. VOCM Radio was broadcasting live from the auditorium Uncle Tim's Barn Dance Troop. Space was tight. Neither Gabriel or Larry had ever attended the facility before. Opened a year earlier to members of the armed forces and the merchant marine, the Knights Of Columbus Hostel was gathering acclaim as a residence, and centre of special events for the military and their friends. The auditorium was packed with Canadian, American, and British members of the armed forces, along with the Newfoundland Militia; all young, exuberant, enjoying fun and youthful camaraderie in wintry old St. John's. Just 20 minutes into the program, at just after 11 P.M., Gabriel Ryan heard noises and fairly loud thuds. Concluding that a fight had erupted in the rear of the packed room, a common occurrence on a Saturday night in old downtown St. John's, he didn't even bother to look around. Until the screeches of "Fire!" reverberated through-out the closed-in walls. He observed the performers on stage throw down their microphones and run. He ran too, through the cafeteria and towards the main door, along with the rushing, pulsating, panicky surge of people who had blindly, futilely attempted to escape through a door that opened in, when it should have opened out. The builders of the Knights of Columbus Canadian Army Huts had reneged on specifications to St. John's Council. They also broke laws by putting in plywood-covered screen doors that opened inward instead of outward. There wasn't a direct exit. The passageway was obstructed from the auditorium to the front street. People wanting to make their way to the front entrance on Harvey Road had to cross a restaurant and canteen packed with loose tables and chairs. As well, there were no separate emergency lighting systems. The unfortunate revellers of the dance party didn't stand a chance.

Bodies , one on top of another, met Gabriel's horrified gaze. People were dropping where they stood, from the incinderous gases. Women with hair and clothes on fire, and blessing themselves while crying and praying, seemed like a terrible nightmare; it couldn't be real. Just a few minutes ago he and his brother and friends were laughingly walking fast along the chilly street, rushing to get inside and get a seat. Now they were all going to die. The place had been bombed he thought. Almost immediately the lights had gone out, adding indescribable terror and confusion to the panic. Gabriel Ryan stood in the choking, gasping, panicking mob, fear slowly paralysing his senses as he realized he might be about to die. The building was now in utter darkness. Bodies were piling up everywhere, and the screams were horrible, as desperate people pounded futilely on locked doors which were proving next to impossible to open by would-be rescuers outside. There was nowhere to find a means of escape. Smoke was overpowering him. He was trapped.

Back in St. Joseph's, Elizabeth Ryan had been on her knees at intervals between her bedroom, parlour, and kitchen the night through. She was praying, with her rosary beads entwined in her tired fingers. She had not slept. The feeling of cold dread around her heart persisted. She was convinced something had happened to her sons. They figured largely in her thoughts, in light of the radio going dead so suddenly. Did she imagine it, or did she hear a woman's panicked scream before the silence? If Larry had been dancing on the program as he said he would, then Gabriel would be in attendance as well. The two brothers loved a bit of fun and music. She was an intuitive lady, who kept up with the news of the world . Just recently, Gabriel had expressed a desire to be deployed overseas. Jim was already seeing action in Africa and Italy. Was she to lose Gabriel and Larry here, on home soil? Those shooting swishes of freezing air that whistled by her like a funnel at the same moment as the station going off the air was a

57

premonition, she felt sure. It portended something terrible.

It was Sunday, early morning. Elizabeth had been praying all night. Now she must go to Mass. She never missed Sunday Mass if she could help it at all. She rose from her knees, swallowed some tea, donned bandanna and coat, and walked slowly up the gravel road to church. It didn't take long for her fears to be founded. Boisterous town crier Sara O'Neill, who wrote the community notes for the church, was blustering towards her, on the hilltop pathway up to the building, exclaiming over the "awful thing" that had transpired in St. John's the night before. The Knights Of Columbus had burned to the ground and there was heavy loss of life! Elizabeth got through Mass in a daze, praying even more intensely. Now she knew the mother's sacrifice. Her heart wrenched with the unbearable pain of loss she felt was coming, her sons Gabriel and Larry burned to death. Friends and neighbours trickled in to her kitchen as the morning progressed, to comfort her. The community waited and prayed until the following afternoon, when a telegram from oldest son Eddie arrived, informing his mother Gabriel and Larry were injured, but alive.

The disaster claimed 99 lives, and injured 109. A Commission Of Inquiry strongly hinted   it to be the actions of German sabotage. But no public inquiry could solve the mystery of just how Elizabeth Ryan knew her sons were in mortal danger. The following factors defy logic, and illustrate unexplainable forces at work: the timeline of her radio going dead from the flames 80 miles away which cut off reception at the source (verbal statements from survivors all agreed *"there was a whistling sound, then the lights went out,")* . *the whistling, rocket-like swishes of air that swept by her legs at the same time as the radio went off , and the whistling sounds when the lights went out. All happening at the same time, shortly after 11 P.M., when the explosive fire was in full force.* Did the psychic power of her entreaties on bended knee save them?   The unseen telegraphy in the sound waves of time and space , even eschewing faith and prayer to the believers, were strong enough to exact a miracle for her two trapped boys, where so many others perished in the flames. (*For complete story of Gabriel Ryan and his dramatic escape and heroism in the Knights Of Columbus Fire, read "His Soldier's Coat: Gabriel Ryan And The Knights Of Columbus Fire Of 1942, " by Shannon M. Lush, Mulberry Books 2017)*

HAUNTING IN THE ATTIC: TWILLINGATE

Twillingate is a town of 2,269 people located on the Twillingate Islands in Notre Dame Bay, Newfoundland. The earliest known people to inhabit the area were the Maritime Archaic, who occupied it in 1500 BC. These were supplanted by the Beothuk, and the Dorset Inuit, until European settlers arrived. These were mostly fishermen and their families from the West Country of England. The town has a long and intriguing history. One of the last known Beothucks on the island of Newfoundland was *Demasduwit,* also called *Shendoreth,* but the priest of the Church Of England, Rev. John Leigh, renamed her *Mary March,* after the Blessed Virgin Mary, and for the month she was kidnapped in. She died on January 08, 1820. *Georgina Stirling* was an opera singer who was born in Twillingate to an illustrious family, and grew there until she was in her 20's. Her stage name was *Marie Toulinquet* (*Toulinquet* being French for Twillingate), and she became a world-renowned prima donna soprano, performing in opera houses throughout Europe and the U.S. in the 1890's. Billed as the Iceberg Capital of the World, Twillingate, once having thrived in the fishing industry until the cod moratorium of 1992, now plies tourism as a flourishing trade. Like many Newfoundland outports, it has stunningly beautiful rugged coastlines, historical, picturesque streets, lush countryside roads. In the waters off the coasts there are whales, dolphins, harp seals, seabirds, and of course, icebergs in season.   There is plenty to attract tourists, with live performances every night including kitchen parties, traditional music sessions, and Dinner Theatre. The Fish, Fun and Folk Festival is a highlight of the tourist season with a rousing time every July.

   With such a rich culture and history of early settlement, more than likely Twillingate is known to house some paranormal/ghostly inhabitants.   The 3 and 4-storey saltbox bed and breakfast houses , with their slanted attic rooms, preserved or restored to their original condition , are the popular choices for visiting tourists if they are lucky enough to book one in time, and don't mind the extra cash for staying in a period house.

   One summer a few years ago, a couple, Bob and Janet Clarke, from St. John's had been unusually busy, and found themselves having to put off their planned trip to Twillingate until very late in the season, the last few days of August. They had visited Twillingate several times, and it stayed on their list of go-to places every few years or so. This particular year, they had even forgotten to book an economical B&B, and just left it to play by ear, as they arrived in the town after a long drive with no stops that afternoon. When they arrived at one of the period inns,   Janet was ecstatic to be told they could have the attic section. After climbing the four flights of stairs, with charming twists and turns, and artsy stuff to look at on every turn, Janet let out a gasp of delight as she discovered they had a whole complete attic section to themselves!

   "Wow, this is awesome!" Janet exclaimed. "It pays to wait until late in the season. Look what we got at the price of a much smaller place! And it's in the attic!" Together they walked around, feasting their eyes. There was a living room, two bedrooms, and an alcove, the beds invitingly arrayed in patchwork quilts and antique homespun lace. The attic looked and smelled like it had recently been done over with new wood, planed and stained to achieve the original look.   But the originality was there, in structure and design, and they loved it. They were both charmed, and Bob remarked he was wishing they had brought some friends. What a party they would have. All that space!   "Gosh," said Janet, looking again through the whimsical round window at the spectacular view so far below. "Look how high we are up. It doesn't go up any further. No one above us, just the sky. We are sleeping at the top tonight!" She happily went in to get ready for Dinner Theatre while Bob made a drink.   "Right beneath the eves!" He said as he took a sip.

The proprietor had loaned the couple the keys to the main door, as he would not be there until the following morning, to prepare breakfast. They assumed there were other guests staying there, but didn't see any evidence of them. They went to the Dinner Theatre at New World Island Theatre, and enjoyed a lovely meal, and entertainment from the skits and musical variety show. After chatting with some friends from previous trips,   they walked back in the quiet night, the activity in the town having slowed considerably with it being late August, but Bob and Janet didn't mind. They were looking forward to getting back to their quaint attic digs, after the long drive out from St. John's that day.

It was rather dark as they walked, and Janet remarked that there wasn't much streetlight. Indeed most of the streetlights seemed to have been turned off, no doubt a cost saving measure, with, again, the tourist rush having slowed down for another season. Most of the houses in the town looked quiet too, and there were few lights on in them. They finally reached the Inn. Janet headed for the alcove, and flopped on the cosy bed, intending to read, as Bob, not as tired, opted for a drink and some junk food as he reclined on the sofa for awhile. He didn't turn the T.V. or radio on, preferring to enjoy the ambiance. Janet heard him go down the stairs presumably to get some ice, and then she dropped off to sleep with all the lights on. She woke up some time later by a sound like heavy hammering. Still half asleep she was surprised to see Bob lying back on the sofa, with a strange look on his face. "What's going on?" She thought he looked a little pale. "I thought you had gone outside for awhile."

"Did you hear it?"

She rubbed her eyes, still confused. "I heard something. Like hammering. It woke me up."

"Didn't you hear the rest of it?"

"Rest of it?"

"The bangings. The voices. All that noise."

"What? I must have died when I slept. Where is it coming from? Is there a party somewhere?"

"That's just it. There is not a soul around. No one is here. No one outside either. I checked. I went out and walked all around the house. No one is around. There's no one working or anything. It's 3 A.M. for God's sake. Everyone is in bed."

"Then what is it? Where are the noises coming from?"

Bob gestured with his head. "Up there. In the roof. Hammering and banging and scraping and grinding, like someone was tearing the place apart. And voices too. It went on for about an hour. I felt sure you would wake up."

"I did hear it. I was just too groggy to wake up. But then I'm a bit away from the living room." Janet looked at Bob. He was bothered, she knew.

She felt a little funny too, but she was just too sleepy to think about it very much, and it had stopped now anyway. "Come on," she said. "Let's go to bed. Lots to do tomorrow, remember." Bob sat up and fidgeted. "I wasn't going to tell you this. But while you were asleep I saw something in the loveseat. A white shadow. It looked like a woman, but it came and went so fast I wasn't sure. I thought it was you, but when I looked you were fast asleep in the alcove."

Janet caught her breath, but it was close to 4 A.M. She thought it best to let reason prevail. "Oh, that was nothing. Just your eyes. You're not wearing your glasses. You know what your vision is like without your glasses. Come on, we had a long day. Let's get some rest." His wife's common sense seemed to mollify Bob and the two settled down. The rest of the night passed okay, with them getting a sound sleep. Next morning, the proprietor and his staff came over to prepare breakfast, and they went down to the dining room, ate a nice meal, and socialized with the other guests for a little while, who were staying in the other Inns owned by the proprietor. Was it just a coincidence of the lateness of the season, or was there a reason why no one but them was staying at their Inn on that particular night? What was the real meaning behind the barrage of loud noises they heard? And did Bob really see a phantom woman sitting on the loveseat? Were there spirits of the early residents of the Inn who were objecting to the renovations in the old attic? Were they in the form of spirit carpenters who were determined to rip off the new wood and stain and put the attic back like it was? Were they long ago dead children of another century who had played in that attic long before it was modernised and glossed over with shellac? Janet thought about that, and she and Bob talked about the great Georgina Stirling, whom she had read about in the museum the next day. Bob remained adamant at what he had heard and seen. Maybe , during the tourist season, with all the singing and activity, she wanted to be a part of it, and the way it used to be, when she visited her childish home on jaunts to Twillingate Island from her star-studded performances in the glittering opera halls of Europe.

THE GHOST ON THE BRIDGE

Conversations and stories casually told in range of one's hearing, whether in the family kitchen, or coffee shop, can settle in your subconscious, and produce activity in the imagination. This may explain what happened to a young teen, Baxter Noonan, on a dark drive to his rural home from St. John's one night in the 1960's. Baxter, on his first job, had just bought his first car, and being proud of it, was enjoying the drive to his home, with the intention of showing it off to his family and friends. He was on the last leg of the trip, and had to cross a bridge over an age-old treacherous cliff, which , he thought to himself, he would never want to be unfortunate enough to topple over, into the gurging falls below. With no streetlights and muted lights from only a scattered house, the lonely road was dark. Baxter turned his lights on high beam, and proceeded to cross the bridge. Suddenly, directly in his view, leaning against the plank on the end of the bridge, was a woman. She was ghostly pale, in old-fashioned clothes, and seemed transparent. Baxter was bewildered and not a little scared. He couldn't believe it was a ghost, but who was it? It didn't seem human. His heart started to beat fast and he wondered what to do. How could he get past her? He was shaking by this time, and decided he just couldn't drive past her while looking at her, he would end up off the bridge into the gushing torrent below, and drown for sure. He closed his eyes, gave a sharp shot to the accelerator, praying he would get across, and that she would be gone when he opened them again. When he got across, he opened his eyes and there was no sign of the phantom. Just as he was beginning to get his breath back, he realised he had yet to pass the graveyard a few miles down! Needless to say, Baxter had a harrowing ride home, but made it. When he went to bed, he lay awake trying to process what he had seen, He hadn't spoken of it to his family. Then, into his mind flashed a memory of a story he had heard his mother tell, but which he hadn't paid too much attention to. It had been a few years, but the details suddenly came back to him. Back in the 1930's , few people had cars in rural areas, and a goodly number of people still used horse and buggy or horse and dray to get around. It was winter, and icy. In Catholic communities in Newfoundland, it was considered lazy and lawless to miss Mass. A man and his wife were travelling from one community to another to Mass, a distance of some 18 miles. They were afraid to be late, and seemingly urged the horse to go faster. The horse slipped on the ice on the bridge, and all ended up in the rushing torrents below. They were killed. A cold sweat broke out on Baxter's brow, as the details of his mother's story became clearer. It was the same bridge! Had he seen the ghost of the tragic woman? Perhaps, perhaps not. His overactive imagination from the darkness and isolation nearing the bridge could have conjured up the story from the depths of his subconscious and produced the image. Or, the unfortunate woman could have been still wandering the earth, lamenting her untimely and horrific passing.

SHE WALKS AT MIDNIGHT IN HIGH HEELS

I heard this story many times from a now elderly friend   whose name is changed here. She was a lady who loved the sounds and scents of nature while she retired for the night with a favourite book. She lived in a two-storey frame house in a rural area just outside of Clarenville, Newfoundland, with her family , a husband and several children. The house was very close to the only road through the community, and spaced meadows apart from the other houses, as in a typical Newfoundland outport.   On quiet summer nights when you could almost hear a pin drop on the road outside her window, she loved to read upstairs in her room, with the wide-silled window up,   indulging in the fragrance of her garden lilacs, and listening to the frogs croak to each other from the pond across the road. One beautiful, starry August night in the 1960's,   quiet and still, with not a breeze or breath of wind, the lady whom I'll call Bernadette was enjoying her solitude in her room , reading as usual. Her husband was away, working. Her children were in bed. The window was as usual, open. It was about 2 A.M. After awhile, she plainly heard what sounded like clicking footsteps passing hurriedly by outside on the paved road. The clicking intrigued her, because it seemed to be coming from high heeled shoes, indeed from spike-heeled shoes, so refined was the sound. Curious as to who this trendy woman might be, and where she was going at such an hour, Bernadette got up and went to the window. She looked down at the road below her. No one was there. She craned her neck to look up and down the road. Not a soul was in sight. But the clicking continued, the determined and confident assured walk of a woman with a destination in mind, as she briskly walked past the house time and again. Bernadette, surprised but assuming she must have turned in somewhere, but doubting it, resumed her sitting position on her chair and commenced her reading again. Suddenly, the high-heeled clicking started up again, back and forth, back and forth underneath the window. She got up and went to the window again. No one was to be seen.   Feeling unnerved at this point, she abandoned the reading, and went down to the kitchen to put on the teapot. All her family was in bed. She would not awaken them for what had to be a figment of her imagination.   She stayed downstairs until she got too sleepy, then went back to her room. Gingerly she got into bed, but kept the light on. The clicking had stopped. She never did hear it again, and simply referred to it as her "strange but true unexplained experience."

THE GHOST IN THE CELL PHONE

iphones and cell phones of all makes and options have become as necessary a tool to our daily lives as a set of keys is to our cars. And not just a necessity, but a tool for entertainment as well, with the rise of social media. Brian Haynes, from Corner Brook, was a busy young man who studied at MUN and was also holding down a job at Walmart. Between his full course study load, his job, and social life, he had little time for playing with apps on his cell phone. He used the internet when time allowed, in and out personal calls/texts and the scattered photo on impulse of a nice sunset. That was the extent of his cell phone scrolling. No one could accuse him of being your run of the mill internet nerd. That is what makes the following story a somewhat chilling one.

About a year ago, something happened with Brian's cell phone which he was unable to explain. "It was creepy, I can tell you that," He says. "I just can't explain it." Brian had come home from a night shift at Walmart, threw his phone, screen down, on the counter in the long kitchen, and headed for the sofa to watch some T.V. before he went to sleep. That was his plan. He never made it to the T.V. watching, since he fell asleep almost right away. He woke up six hours later, and going to the kitchen, prepared to charge his phone. The phone was laying where he had left it, uncharged, the battery having been used up. He needed to check with a friend about the schedule for one of the MUN courses he was taking. When he picked it up, he recoiled in shock and horror at what he saw. There, on the screen he was looking at a crystal clear photo of himself, sound asleep on the sofa. This creeped him out enough, but to the left of the photo was an image of an elderly man gazing down at him while he slept. Brian was not only grossed out, but mystified. The phone had been turned upside down, it was uncharged, no battery "juice" whatsoever in it. The living room was a good distance away from the long kitchen, and the phone high up on the counter; thus it was impossible for the phone to focus or self-capture from the physical distance and layout.

Brian made himself some coffee, and took a shower to try and clear his head. When he emerged from the shower, and went to check the now charged phone, the chilling photo was still there on the screen. He was looking at himself sound asleep on the sofa, lying on his back. The creepy elderly man gazed down on him from behind the sofa. Brian felt shivers going through him. "I hope to hell it deletes," he said to himself as he went to the options. Luckily it did. The image was no longer there, but it stuck in Brian's mind for a few days. He thought of asking the landlord about the history of the place, if any old men had lived there at any time, but he decided to just leave it be. He had a busy life; he didn't need the hassle. But it wasn't related , he told himself a few days later, when he threw the phone in the trash and picked out a new one. "I needed a new one anyway," he quipped, and thereafter never mentioned, or thought about, the unsettling incident again.

TERROR IN A WHITE HORSE

White horses are portrayed in mythology in many cultures of the world. They can be divinatory, who prophesy , or warn of danger. In the New Testament, the Four Horsemen of the Apocalypse include one seated on a white horse (pestilence), while the "pale" carried the rider, Death. In Biblical times white horses were associated with battle ("Christ rides a white horse to judge and make war upon the earth." (Book of Revelations). In Norse folklore its appearance was a definite symbol of death. Some symbols of meaning white horses have in varying cultures include: Pride, Nobility, War, Freedom, Independence, Life and Death, Fertility, Power, Lust and Sexuality, Travel, Pathway to and from the Underworld, plus the higher realms in Celtic and Greek Mythology.

In the mindset of the people from the community where the following story is set, seeing a white horse could only mean one thing: instant death.

In the 1930's in Ferryland , a town in the Irish Loop of the Avalon Peninsula, one night a man named Bill O'Connor , not his real name, carelessly left his home in the middle of the Rosary being said (an unheard of act in a devoutly Catholic home of those years!), and walked up the road. "I haven't time to bother with the Rosary now," he shot back at his mother as he went out the door. "I'm going." He walked some distance, and soon came to where he had to cross a bridge. As he attempted to cross the bridge, a huge white horse with a huge man atop it, came across the bridge and stopped , horse and rider staring him down, as if daring him to move any further. Bill O'Connor nearly dropped where he stood. The White Horse. Death. He was going to die! He turned around and rushed back home, expecting at any second to be struck down , sure he was breathing his last breath. When he went in the door, he fell on the floor, shocking the assembled group who were still on their knees, immersed in the Five Sorrowful Mysteries. Bill had what only can be ascribed to a breakdown , spending three months in bed, waiting to die, with the priest attending to him , from his terror at seeing the death token, the White Horse. Bill didn't die, but his terror of seeing the ghostly White Horse haunted his dreams for the rest of his natural-born days.

THE BLACK BLANKET

In many and varying cultures and religions, including Christianity, a black blanket thrown in one's pathway is perceived to be demonic, or evil. In traditional societies, the idea could be connected to the fact that the departed is covered with a blanket, or shroud. Seeing a black blanket could mean you are seeing someone's burial cloth shroud, or gravecloth. Or, the experience of seeing the black blanket could mean something as simple, or similar to, as seeing a black cat cross your path: black cats walking in front can mean good luck, walking away bad luck or no luck at all, since they are taking the luck with them. But invariably, seeing a black blanket is usually perceived as a warning, that something is about to happen, and that something is not good.

One night during the 1930's, Jerome Ryan, Senior, was walking home from visiting a relative. There was a windswept moon, and stars out, which took away some of the inky darkness prevalent on a moonless night in the then village devoid of electric lights. He was walking on a gravel road, the only road through the community, and he had walked about a half mile before he was suddenly stopped by a strange sight. A massive black blanket was spread across the road, from one side to the other. Jerome could not get to cross it. He attempted several times to cross the road, but the weird shroud stopped him. He would manage to put one foot ahead, then was immediately blocked from moving any further. He turned around a couple of times, wondering what to do, pondering if he should go back down to his relative's house, but his wife and family were expecting him at home. By this time he was starting to feel a little nervous, since he had never encountered anything like this before. Just as he had made up his mind to go back down the road from where he left, and get someone to walk home with him, a whirlwind whipped up in the otherwise calm night. The black blanket went on up in the air. He was able to walk on freely. Jerome told the story to interested listeners through the years, but admitted that at that time, he knew no significance of a black blanket being any kind of warning, or anything else. If he had, he would undoubtedly have handled it with not as much ease or finesse as he did.

SAVED BY A DEAD FATHER'S VOICE

Much has been written about , documented and researched concerning the Old Hag syndrome. This phenonemon , known only to Newfoundland as the Old Hag , the name having been watered down in other cultures, has as its most extreme elements a person sitting on the chest of the victim; rape; a ghost or apparition getting in bed with the victim, among many other horrible attacks. The antidotes practiced for preventing this gruesome ordeal were just as horrific, among them driving nails in a piece of clapboard and wearing the board to bed strapped to one's chest! Growing up in St. Mary's Bay, Newfoundland, I knew only that when someone had the Old Hag, they couldn't come awake, and one of the methods used to help the victim was to count backwards , or say the Lord's Prayer over the victim until the victim came awake. I heard nothing about ugly, gnarled old women sitting on victim's chests, or wearing a nail-pierced board to bed. Had I heard such things, chances are I would be having a goodly number of nightmares myself! The Old Hag in my neck of the woods was spoken of in casual terms: "My God B'y, I had the old hag last night. Not too bright today...." etc. etc. I never did hear anything as extreme or horrific as the literature I discovered later in my readings on the subject. I did hear several stories on the experience, my grandfather having experienced it a few times, though as mentioned, certainly not as horrific. A relative woke up one night many years ago in a small town,   suffering from sleep paralysis, to see a woman in period clothes and a high hat standing at the foot of his bed. I also heard some modern stories, and am presenting one here. The subject did not experience someone sitting on her chest, rather a tightening of her chest so she couldn't breathe. She didn't experience smells or sounds. She could see everything around her but she couldn't move, couldn't wake up, couldn't get out of bed.

Theresa Parody of Goose Bay, who was recently divorced, and whose father had died recently, had had a stressful few weeks with work when she went to bed one night in 2008. Sometime around 3 A.M. she opened her eyes, but was unable to breathe or move. She could see everything around her, the lights left on in her room, every detail of the objects on her bureau, night table, clothes in her closet. She seemed to get up and walk out to the living room but in reality she was not able to move. Inexplicably, she somehow saw herself walking out the hallway and into the living room. On the bed, she was desperately trying to come to her senses, but just could not come fully awake, her eyes wide open, aware of everything around her, but her arms and limbs in a paralysed state. She could see her ensuite bathroom with the light on, she could see everything in her room. But her brain could not tell her muscles and limbs to get up off the bed. It felt like she was glued to the bed. She lay there helpless. Her mind was saying, "I have to get up. I have to get up before I die," as she was becoming increasingly more breathless and was struggling to get air. She could see her phone on the bedside table, and wanted to call her boyfriend, but couldn't move her hand to reach it. She tried to call out, even though there was no one to hear her, but could just barely open her mouth and chew at the air like a guppie; no sound would come. Just as she thought she couldn't go on any longer, and she would suffocate to death, she heard her father, who had died a few months before, calling out to her from the wall on the side where she was lying.

He was calling in a firm but gentle voice, "Theresa, Theresa, Theresa." "That's all he said," She remembers. "Just my name. But it was the way he said it, slow, meaningful, every syllable pronounced, and clear, real, not a whisper. It was so reassuring, as if to tell me not to worry, don't panic, you are going to be all right." After a few more repeated callings of her name by whom she believes was her father's spirit, Theresa finally woke up. "I came to fully. I couldn't believe I was really okay. I could still hear my father's voice in my head. But he was gone, he had come to save me, and then he was gone. I got up, everything was the same as I had seen it while I was sleep paralysed, or whatever it was that happened to me. I guess it was the Old Hag. I walked out to the living room and it looked exactly the same as when I left my body and walked out only a few moments before. I stayed up, had some tea, and tried to watch T.V. for awhile. I slept okay the rest of the night. But it was definitely my father's voice, that was not a nightmare. It was his voice, the same as when he was here. I totally believe that. I would swear on any Bible. He had come to save my life that night, because if he hadn't, I think I would truly have died of a heart attack."

THE STOLEN CHILD: A FAIRY STORY

Belief in fairies is strong in the Celtic revival. The extolled Irish writer and poet W.B. Yeats wrote prolifically on his own experiences with the *sidhe* (Irish fairies) and waxed voluminously of their nature and behavior. His colleagues and great Irish Victorian folklorists , including Lady Gregory of the Cuchulain legends (which the Pulitizer-Prize winning Irish writer Frank McCourt remembered so vividly in his memoir), proudly and without secrecy acknowledged their fairy hauntings and sightings. Given the infusion of Irish culture in Newfoundland's DNA, no wonder the mysteries of the little people, the good people, gnomes, elves, leprechauns or just simply humanoids have such strong presence here. However, having said that, usually, with maybe few exceptions, the types of fairies prevalent in our history have been that of the Pied Piper variety: 12-13" high, dancing around a misty pond, or hidden in a cozy tree nook ready to entice a blueberry picker or trouter with their seductive music, and having lured the unsuspecting victims, then lead them to the edge of a cliff. If the victim, in his ecstatic trance, is not stopped in time by another who knows the dangerous cycle, dire and deadly consequences can occur. The even more evil types of fairies steal babies from their cribs, replacing them with an ugly subhuman creature, and afflict with fairy blasts. In my books *Hannigan's Hand,* and *Hannigan's Hand: The Ghost Woman Talks,* young Dan Hannigan, as part of the curse from the headless spirit whose path he had invaded, is struck by a fairy blast so severe that it warrants an exorcism from a priest.

The taking of the fairies syndrome was used regularly as a matter of course in Newfoundland of the past, to keep children safe from wandering and out after dark. Everyone has heard or experienced the bread-in-the-pocket antidote, turning the clothes inside out, coins in the baby's crib, the warning to "go home before the fairies get you, and not to dare pay attention to strange music , indeed listen for it, and not to follow it for any reason, as surely it would be the fairies trying to lure you away."   The wild mushrooms which grew so abundantly in the woods were another hazard: don't step on them or disturb them. Walk over them, as they are fairy caps; places where the fairies dwell. These beliefs and warnings were not idle threats, although it's not likely the innocent people giving them were aware of their dark history.   They had their origins in terror-stricken and ingrained fears of centuries ago, passed down. In some parts of Ireland, Brittany and Germany, there were fairies or spirit paths that while being invisible, had such perceived geographical reality, in the minds of country people, that building practices were adapted to ensure they were not obstructed. It was believed that a dwelling built on a fairy path would suffer supernatural manifestations, and ill luck with animals and personal illness. The consequences of blocking fairy paths were dire. In Ireland especially, people who had illnesses or other misfortunes were said to have blocked a fairy or spirit path. Often, sick children died as a punishment for their father making a house extension where fairies reside. They were "in the way," or "in a contrary place."   Clearly, the old Irish cleric of the Thomas Mackey curse with his "never block a beaten path" mantra was not just a dotty old seer practicing the devil's cures; he was representing lifetime traditions set down in his birth culture as believable and true. (refer to *Hannigan's Hand, Mulberry Books 2015, a horror novel built around the true "blocking the path curse" of Thomas Mackey).*

Gabriel Ryan Senior told a true story of a young girl's capture by   fairies in the community of Colinet, St. Mary's Bay, which happened sometime in his youth, possibly in the mid 1930's. This fairy was not the garden-type diminutive creature, but a normal-looking beautiful woman, who charmingly abducted the girl from her yard by lifting her over the fence. The girl was gone for two weeks, and had the community out with search parties, fearing the worst. Finally she was found, sitting on a rock in a gravel pit, virtually unharmed. However, she could not remember anything about her captivity by the benevolent creature, only that "there was a nice woman, a lovely woman, who had her , and used to bring her around."   The girl was "never the same after," staying true to the notions of the fairies' touch, be they evil, good, big or small, beautiful or ugly.   They were up to no good.

THE FETCH

A fetch is an apparition or double of a living person, the appearance of which often portends death or disaster. Fetches or spirits are annoyingly familiar at sea. Usually if someone on land is about to die, that person's fetch will appear as a signal to a loved one who is on a ship. Also, the spirits of sailors who have drowned or met with some fatal mishap while on the same ship as the one now in operation, will appear as a fetch and try to extract the captain from the wheel, attempting to take over the ship. A person may see his own fetch. A fetch may be seen day or night, usually before or after a person dies. To see someone's fetch from midnight to noon was a sign that that person would soon die. To see someone's fetch from noon to midnight was a sign that person had a long life. In Irish folklore, the name means simply that the phantom is fetching or taking, the soul of the living. In modern times, the same concept is referred to as a *Doppelganger*, a double or look-alike of a living person. It is known to be a harbinger of bad luck, illness or death, for anyone who sees their own double, or that of a loved one.

Perhaps there is something about priests, or clergy, that invites spirit energy. This story comes from a woman whose grandmother worked for a priest in a Newfoundland rural community many years ago as a housekeeper. She had worked for him for a few years, and certainly would not mistake him for someone else. One evening she had cooked his supper, and had it in the oven warming up for when he came in and was ready to partake. When she saw him in his study, she brought the supper in to him, as he had directed her to do. On her way, she saw him open the door and come out. He went on to the front door, and his soutanne (long black day garment), got caught in the door. He loosened it, pulled it out and kept on going. She brought back the meal and put it in the warmer again. She waited for awhile, and hearing noises, assumed he was back again, and brought in the meal. "Father," she said. "I was in you know, and I saw you going out. So I brought back your meal, and put it in to warm for you."

"Me go out?" The priest said. "I was never out."

"Yes, Father," The housekeeper said. "Sure I saw you; the door got caught up in your soutanne and you cleared it."

"Haw," He said. "I hope he didn't take my money, but I was never out of here."

Luckily for him, his fetch appeared to the housekeeper at the supper hour, within the noon to midnight time frame, which forebode the happy tidings that foretold a long life. The housekeeper also enjoyed a long life, with no ill effects, on having witnessed the doppleganger double of her laconic employer.

Phone Call From The Other Side

Ghosts and paranormal happenings can make a lot of people uncomfortable, especially in these modern times. Most people don't want to attest to the fact they believe in any of it, although they may find it fascinating, even entertaining. As long as they are not the ones who witness something out of the ordinary. The following are two stories of loved ones returning to say goodbye after they died. They could be perceived as incidents of crisis apparitions. Crisis apparitions are the spirits or voices, often over distance, of a recently deceased person who visits a loved one they had a close connection with in life, to say a final goodbye. The first, tragic and sad, happened recently in Labrador, the second years ago in Carbonear.   Some say they are guardian angels; others say they are a trick of the brain, that people in mourning   unconsciously produce apparitions to console themselves after losing a loved one. Whatever the scientific diagnosis, to someone who has seen or heard a real loved one in apparition form after the death of that loved one, no one can convince them it was their imagination. They quickly cross over from the skeptic to the believer, and there's no going back.

Sheila's Story:

Sheila Gainor , from a community in Labrador, (not her real name), wrote to me   that she had never given paranormal activity of any kind a second thought, until she had what she later found out to be possibly a crisis

77

apparition after the death of Brittany, her daughter, some thirty years before. Brittany was hit by the travel bug from the time she was a child. When she was a university student, she would travel all over the world, and work to help with her tuition, and to soak up the culture. She loved to meet new people, and was constantly coming and going, changing places and bed-sitters as fast as she changed her socks. Sheila supported her choices, but worried about her travelling so much alone.   One spring, Brittany, following her final semester for her Phd, decided to spend a few weeks in London, England, prior to her accepting a position at a local hospital as an intern. She had worked at a high- end restaurant all winter part-time to pay the fare, and supplement the funds from her student loans.

 A week after Brittany arrived in London, Sheila got a late night phone call. It was 4 A.M. The line was staticy, but she could clearly hear Brittany's voice. Excitedly she asked her how she was. It didn't occur to her that anything was wrong, which was strange, she said, since she was always worrying about her safety in strange cities all over the globe.   "Mom, " said Brittany, "I just wanted to tell you that I'm really happy, and that I love you. Don't worry about me. I'll be alright. Goodbye." Then the phone went dead. Sheila was perplexed, but figured it was just the line having problems, given all the static. Or that Brittany was out somewhere with some friends and impulsively called her. She often did that, and at strange hours, but the calls were never as short or ended so abruptly as this one. She tried to not worry, but she couldn't sleep.

 At noon the next day, a Royal Newfoundland Constabulary Officer came to her door. When she saw him, she braced for the worst. He told her, white-faced, that her daughter Brittany had been in an accident. She was dead. She had been struck by a drunk driver in London the night before and died instantly. The next few weeks of bringing Brittany's body home, the funeral and aftermath was a   blur. It was a couple of months before Sheila allowed herself to really think about Brittany's last phone call to her, and what she had said. She remembered the time, close to 4 A.M. She had just assumed the accident had happened shortly after she had talked to her. One day she called the RNC, and asked to be put through to the officer who had come to her with the shocking news. She told him she wanted information from forensics in London as to the exact time Brittany's accident had happened, and the exact moment she died. He got back to her the next day. What he told her changed her forever, and challenged all her preconceived notions about the spiritual bond between loved ones.   From the information on file in forensics in England , accurate to the fraction of a second, Brittany had been struck by a drunk driver driving a lorry while she crossed Charing Cross Road. She was killed instantly. The time of death was recorded at 7 A.M., London time, 4 A.M. St. John's time, 30 minutes before she had called Sheila.

He Wants To Tell You He's O.K

Diane's Story

I had been very close to my father all my life.   I grew up in Gander, and moved to Carbonear when I got married. Dad and Mom stayed with my husband and me whenever they came to St. John's. They always slept in the spare room. When Dad was 81, he was admitted to the Health Sciences Centre for dizzy spells. They kept him in longer than any of us expected, and his health worsened, I think because of the anxiety he had over hospitals. He just wanted to go home, but they wouldn't let him out, only kept doing test after test after test. My mother and siblings and myself took turns being by his bedside. After he had been there a few weeks I went over to see him, promising him I would be back later that night. Everyone said he was doing better, so I decided to wait until the next day. Around 2:30 that night a call came. The family had to go to the hospital. It was urgent. We all rushed down. He had taken a turn for the worse, and had had a massive stroke while he slept. He was gone. I was shattered, devastated. What hurt so much was that he had died alone, only a few hours after my siblings had said goodnight and gone home. They said he seemed fine, or they would not have left. I was grief-stricken for awhile, and feeling guilty that I had not gone down a second time that evening. A few weeks after he died, I was in the spare room, getting ready for bed. I had picked the spare room since my bedroom was being painted. It was a steaming hot night, something like 34 Celsius. Suddenly the room began to get cold. The bed was freezing, I could feel the mattress beneath me turn cold like a lump of ice. Thinking there had been a rapid change in the weather, that the fog had rolled in, I got up and looked through the window. The sky was still in a heat haze, and people were outside on their decks having a late night cold drink in their T-shirts and shorts. I came out to the kitchen, and soon had to up the air conditioning, the air was so warm. I went back to the spare room, got in bed, and felt the freezing chill again. The sheets were like ice, the mattress was icy like before. It was a clammy kind of cold, hard to explain, not really dampness, but going right in through my bones. I was shivering. There was also a cold draft all through the room.

As I went to get up again, I noticed a photo lying face up on my bedside table. As soon as I noticed it I felt warm again and a wonderful feeling of joy went right in through me. I gasped in astonishment and delight. It was a childhood photo of me and my father that I had been looking for for decades, since I was a young teenager. It was the only photo I had of my father, with me in it. I was about three, and he had me by the hand as we walked on the street. It was like gold to me, and it had become lost, I thought forever. There it was! Where did it come from! All of a sudden like that! It hadn't been there before, I was certain. Suddenly I felt a sense of peace. I had been feeling guilty over not being there when he died. No one should have to die alone. If only I had gone over that evening for the second time. But I think he was trying to tell me something that night, not to feel bad anymore, that he was okay. And his loving energy made certain that picture would end up in the right place, where I would find it. It was his final goodbye and parting gift to me. I think he sent me that picture. I was never able to find it anywhere, it had disappeared for decades. After I had a good cry, I got back into bed, and the room was normal again.

Grandmother Came To Say Goodbye

Gabriel Ryan lived with his nine siblings, his parents, and his grandparents in an 1880's period house in St. Mary's Bay. Though hectic with so many children around, his grandmother Esther seemed to take to Gabriel moreso than the rest. When Gabriel left home to join the army during WW2, she missed him. While he was in the army she passed away. Unable to make it home to the wake and funeral, he managed to visit home a few weeks after she died. One evening , the family were saying the Rosary around the supper table. The table was in front of the kitchen window, and Gabriel had a clear view of anyone walking up and down the lane from where he was sitting. He was about three feet from the window, when he happened to glance and saw his grandmother, a tiny elderly woman with a shawl wrapped around her head, the same as when she was alive, pass the window, look in, and then disappear. "I was not afraid or nervous at all," he said. "When the Rosary was over, I told my mother a woman had passed up the lane but didn't come in. I knew it was my grandmother; she just came by to say goodbye to me."

Background References And Sources:

Dictionary Of Newfoundland English (C 71-95)

-Heritage Of Newfoundland And Labrador

-Encyclopedia Of Newfoundland And Labrador. Harry Cuff Publications. 1994

-Library And Archives Canada

-Fairy And Folk Tales Of The Irish Peasantry . W.B. Yeats 1888

-The Celtic Twilight W.B. Yeats 1902

-The Terror That Comes In The Night . David J. Hufford . Copyright 1982. University Of Pennsylvania Press

-His Soldier's Coat: Gabriel Ryan And The Knights Of Columbus Fire Of 1942. Copyright Shannon Marshall Lush. Mulberry Books. 2017

-True Irish Ghost Stories Compiled By St. John D. Seymour and Harry L. Neligan Copyright 1974 . Causeway Books

-A Treasury Of Irish Myth, Legend, And Folklore W.B. Yeats . Arvenal Books 1986

Hannigan's Hand: A Ghost Novel. Geraldine Ryan-Lush, Mulberry Books, 2013

-Hannigan's Hand: The Ghost Woman Talks Geraldine Ryan-Lush, Mulberry Books 2015

About The Author

Geraldine Ryan-Lush was born and raised in St. Joseph's, St. Mary's Bay, Newfoundland, Canada. She received a B.A.(ED) from Memorial University, majoring in English Language/Literature, and taught school in St. Mary's Bay, Goose Bay/Labrador, Gambo, St. John's, Mount Pearl, and Manitoba. She began her writing career as a columnist for The Evening Telegram and The NL Herald. She has been published by traditional publishers as Annick Press, Toronto/NY, Borealis Press, Ottawa, Breakwater Books, Mulberry Books. She is author to date of 16 books, ranging from picture books to adult novels to a collection of adult poetry. She has also published numerous scholarly articles on the children's literature field, in sources as Books In Canada, The Newfoundland Quarterly, and Canadian Children's Literature. Her books have been widely reviewed in sources as School Library Journal, N.Y., Canadian Book Review Annual, Canadian Children's Literature, Quill&Quire, The Toronto Star, Winnipeg Free Press, Copley News Services, Washington, DC, The Evening Telegram, CBC Radio, Rogers Cable, many others. Her books, some in translation, have been on the American Bookseller's Pick of the Lists, received the Merit Magazine Studio Award, Alcuin Society Design Award, Readers' Favourite 5-Star Award (honored by the American Library Association), and Atlantic Books Today Editors' Pick. She lives in Mount Pearl, NL.

Titles By Geraldine Ryan-Lush:

-*The Gravel Pit Kids (Young Adult Novel)*

-*The Seashell's Lament (Adult Novel)*

-*Mrs. Clohiggledy's Clutter (All Ages)*

-*Hannigan's Hand (Paranormal Novel, YA-Adult)*

-*Hannigan's Hand: The Ghost Woman Talks* (Paranormal Novel, YA-Adult)

-*No Go Potty* (Chapter Book, Malcolm K. Wall Series)

-*Malcolm The Klutz* (Chapter Book, Malcolm K. Wall Series)

-*Malcolm And The Hamster Lady* (Chapter Book, Malcolm K. Wall Series)

-*Once When I Wasn't Looking* (Poetry Collection, Adult)

-*Hairs On Bears* (Picture Book)

-*Jeremy Jeckles Hates Freckles* (Picture/Storybook)

-*Poils Poils Et Repoils* (Picture Book)

-*The Law-Breaking Adventures Of Teacher Tabitha* (Middle Grade. All Ages Appeal

-*Goodbye Wart!* (Rhyming Picture Book)

-*Haunted Towns: Ghost Stories Of Newfoundland and Labrador.* (Non-Fiction Collection Of True Ghost Stories From Across Newfoundland/Labrador)

Coming In 2019: *Jacqueline: A Novel.* (Adult)

----

www.mulberrybooks.com *Facebook: Author GeraldineRyanLush*

Twitter: @GRyanLush Available From: www.amazon.com. www.amazon.ca www.amazon.co.uk www.chapters.indigo.ca www.barnes&noble.com

To order directly and save on prices and shipping contact: geraldine1942 @live.com Telephone: 709.368.5156. Mulberry Books . 27-A Pasadena Crescent. Suite 204 . St. John's, NL Canada A1E 4S4

www.ingramcontent.com/pod-product-compliance
Lightning Source LLC
Chambersburg PA
CBHW071746090426
42738CB00011B/2579